## PRAISE FOR *SEARCHING FOR PETER PALAGI*

The book was a telling story. It shows the strength of dedication and passion.

—*Don Grebien, Mayor of Pawtucket*

Arteaga's *Searching for Peter Palagi* is not your typical historical autobiography. Reading this story is like having a conversation with a friend, whose enthusiasm for Palagis Ice Cream and their overall zest for life and finding happiness through simple pleasures shines so bright, it's contagious.

This book not only celebrates one man's legacy, it gives you an inside look at what kept this beloved brand on the map for 125 years, thanks to Arteaga's shared vision with Palagi for working hard and consistently for the good of the community.

It serves as a step-by-step guide to understand this history while opening your heart to the pure magic that ice cream brings to the hearts of children and adults alike.

—*LuzJennifer Martinez, Deputy Editor,*
The Valley Breeze

When Alex informed me he was writing a book on the comprehensive history of Palagis Ice Cream Company born, raised and still flourishing in Pawtucket, I told him, "You nailed it! This story has never been told, and it's about time it should be. Pawtucket and the surrounding communities will revel in it!"

I knew about Palagis when I was growing up in south Seekonk in the early and mid 1970s. I remember the hot summer afternoons behind the elementary school playing softball with a bunch of buddies and hearing the bells of good ol' Palagis Ford Model A truck ringing out, calling, "You want to cool off? I've got ice cream, popsicles, slush and more!" It was too good to be true.

The memories resonate in my mind, and Alex brings those back to life with his chapters, from how Peter Palagi immigrated to the United States, discovered what he wanted to do for a career, founded the business and made it a success story with his sons later carrying the torch.

He speaks of how he went from being an "ice cream man" as a young adult to eventually owning the business in 1999, his trials and tribulations over the years, the importance of his beloved neighbors—the former Pawtucket Red Sox and McCoy Stadium—and his desire to continue the legend of Palagis Ice Cream.

It's a stellar, heartfelt read for anyone who used to adore, and/or continues to do so, the cool, satisfying products provided by the historic company.

Enjoy!

—*Jon Baker, Journalist,*
*The Blackstone Valley Call & Times*
*(formerly* The Pawtucket Times*)*

I truly enjoyed reading the story of Peter Palagi as it brought back nice childhood memories of the excitement of hearing the ice cream truck bell ringing in the neighborhood and how wonderful it was to have an ice cream cone on a hot summer day at the local baseball field. The author Alex Arteaga has truly honored and preserved Peter Palagi's great legacy for Rhode Islanders to continue to enjoy."

—*Jim Briden, Longtime member of the*
*Pawtucket Business Community*

Our great grandfather, grandfather and father passed their family and business acumen right along to continue its success. That is the Palagis Ice Cream legacy. The immigrant experience and small business ownership are a forged part of America's landscape. When someone takes the time to delve into the history and the essence of a family business and its changing times, it is truly an honor. Alex has taken the helm and his words are a tribute to more than 125 years of service to our communities. It is a triumph he should be proud of.

—*Connie Palagi, granddaughter of Peter Palagi and daughter of Donald Palagi*

This lovingly told story of Palagis Ice Cream Company captures more than a company—it captures a feeling. Born from the dreams of Italian immigrant Peter Palagi—hailed as the father of the American ice cream truck—this Rhode Island treasure began with horse-drawn wagons jingling through cobblestone streets in 1896, bringing cool delight to eager children. For generations, the Palagi name was stitched into the fabric of neighborhood summers, each yellow truck a rolling memory of laughter and sweetness. When Alex Arteaga, another immigrant with a dream, took the reins, he didn't just revive a business—he rekindled a legacy. This book is a scoop of history, a swirl of tradition, and a tribute to the timeless joy of a cold treat on a warm day.

—*Herb Weiss, Author of* Taking Charge: Collected Stories on Aging Boldly, *and two sequels.*

# SEARCHING FOR PETER PALAGI

*"AN AMERICAN LEGEND"*

AMERICA'S FIRST ICE
CREAM MAN AND
FATHER OF THE ICE
CREAM TRUCK

## ALEJANDRO ARTEAGA

Visit our website at **www.StillwaterPress.com** for more information.

First Stillwater River Publications Edition.

ISBN: 978-1-965733-69-1

Library of Congress Control Number: 2025907763

1 2 3 4 5 6 7 8 9 10
Written by Alejandro Arteaga.
Photographs provided by Alejandro Arteaga.
Cover & interior book design by Matthew St. Jean.
Published by Stillwater River Publications, West Warwick, RI, USA.

Publisher's Cataloging-in-Publication
Provided by Cassidy Cataloguing Services, Inc.

Names: Arteaga, Alejandro, 1966- author.
Title: Searching for Peter Palagi : America's first ice cream man and father of
the ice cream truck / Alejandro Arteaga.
Description: First Stillwater River Publications edition. | West Warwick, RI,
USA : Stillwater River Publications, [2025]
Identifiers: LCCN: 2025907763 | ISBN: 9781965733691
Subjects: LCSH: Palagi, Peter. | Businesspeople--Rhode Island--Biography. |
Street vendors--Rhode Island--Biography. | Ice cream industry--Rhode Island--
History. | Ice cream trucks--Rhode Island--History. | Pawtucket (R.I.)--History. |
Rhode Island--Biography. | LCGFT: Biographies.
Classification: LCC: F85 .A78 2025 | DDC: 974.504092--dc23

# DEDICATION

The story of Peter Palagi is the story of an immigrant family coming to America in the late 19th century (1896) and figuring it out, finding their way and making their contributions to their community. Peter's story is not an immigrant story but an American story, as everyone's American story started out as an immigrant's story; you may have to go back a few generations in your family tree to pinpoint exactly where it all began for you and your family, your American story.

In the late 1960's American companies would recruit skilled workers from Colombia's textile industry. They would offer legal immigrant status and a work contract.

My immigrant American story began in the 1970's when in 1972 my father came to Rhode Island with a work contract to work in a textile mill recruited by an American company. Two years later in 1974 my two oldest brothers joined my father with the goal in mind to work and help my father save enough money to bring the rest of the family here to Rhode Island. The rest of the family included my mom and six other siblings.

Then in the summer of 1976 we arrived in Rhode Island to join my father and my two oldest brothers to begin our journey, our immigrant American story, a time of many mixed feelings and emotions, excited to go this new place that we had heard so much about, yet at the same time dealing with the uncertainty of whether leaving our home and our homeland was the right thing to do. Starting over is never an easy thing.

June 26th 1976, a day full of excitement and anxious anticipation all rolled into one, it was a great day!

I dedicate this book to the people who have been on this journey with me......from the beginning, my parents and my 7 siblings, mom dad and eight children, "**a perfect ten!**"

Ironically enough, a very popular TV series at the time was *Eight Is Enough,* a TV series about the Bradford family who had eight children which ran from 1977 to 1981, the year of my father's passing.

In good times and in bad times, family, these are the people who really know who you are and the ones who you can really count on. Let's first start from the major life changing decision, the decision to move to a different country is not a decision that is made on a whim, it is a decision that is planned years in advance and takes years to realize. My father and my mother decided that it could be of great benefit to the family if we would move to the USA.

After coming to that conclusion they made their plan, focused on that goal and did everything in their power to make that happen. As children you just go with the flow for the most part but now as adults we can look back and appreciate their foresight and admire their focused determination to make it all happen.

After arriving in the USA in the summer of 1976, one big happy family, we had a little over four and a half good years with my father as he passed away in early 1981 from a sudden heart attack at the young age of 49.

## THE INSPIRATION TO CARRY ON

As you can imagine, a devastating event for any family but even more so in this situation especially for my mom, here she was in this new country with eight children and her

*My father*

*My mother on graduation day*

husband passes away. My mom spoke the language but did not have a driver's license. She went on to get her driver's license, though not very enthusiastically as she was afraid to drive but she knew that she had to do what she had to do to carry on. She always had a few different jobs at the time and she decided to go back to school while also keeping her jobs. The car that she got at the time was a yellow Chevy Nova which we all famously remember as "The Taxi". So there was our mom, driving to her different jobs, driving to school, keeping up with her schoolwork while still being a mom to eight children, the daily grind and eventually achieving her goal of graduating from Rhode Island College with a teaching degree at the age of 50, quite an inspiration for all of us to carry on regardless of the obstacles in front of us. She was not only an inspiration to all of us but she was an inspiration to the Colombian community as her story got around with a few newspaper articles and through her work.

Our mom passed away in 2022 on her 85th birthday after a long battle with diabetes and in her later years also battling dementia. In her last couple of years she needed constant supervision. It was now our turn to show our gratitude and our extraordinary appreciation for everything that she did for all of us and everything that she was. In those last couple of years there was always one or two of us with her at all times, every one of her children chipping in to help out and contribute, no one doing any more than anyone else….no one doing any less. Not trying to even out the workload between us all but everyone just wanting to do as much as they could, and then some.

So, this book is dedicated to my family, **Team Arteaga.** As they say in Spanish, "*mi gente*", translation, my people, my mom, my dad and all my siblings, **"the perfect ten"**, my story is their story.

Every family has many stories to tell but one interesting anecdote when it comes to our family that sometimes comes up is that my father's name was Alejandro and my mother's name was Amparo and they named me (their youngest son) Alejandro and they named my sister (their youngest daughter) Luz Amparo, so as the story goes, Alejandro and Amparo started it all and Alejandro and Amparo ended it, the bookends of **"the perfect ten"**. Nobody could ever plan that, that's just the way it turned out.

Last but not least in the dedication of this book, I would also like to dedicate this book to my children, Maxwell and Summer. We should always treat ourselves well and see ourselves as most important, not in a selfish way but we need to take care of ourselves first in order to be healthy and strong to help someone else.

Something happens when you have children, you are no longer the most important, they become the number one

*My family, 2021: the perfect ten...minus one. Our dad*
*passed away at the tender age of 49, in 1981.*

*My kids and me. Palagis Ice Cream Shack*
*in the background on fireworks night.*

and we take a second position. Our most important job now becomes taking care of them and setting a good example by being a good human being. They have witnessed my dedication to my work and my writing of this book, which really hasn't been easy. I had no idea how much work it would be, occasional thoughts of quitting but quitting was not an option. It was very important to carry on and see it through to the end and finish what I started, it's our new job and responsibility, to set a good example in every way.

# CONTENTS

Dedication    *vii*

Introduction    *xv*

Chapter 1    The Early Days    1

Chapter 2    The Role of the Family    8

Chapter 3    New Ownership—A New Chapter in the History of Palagis Ice Cream Company, A New Generation & 4th Generation of Company Ownership    16

Chapter 4    Some Challenging Times—The Plight of Small Business    31

Chapter 5    The Magic of Peter Palagi    51

Chapter 6    The Ice Cream Trucks Today    57

Chapter 7    I Know Where I Am... How Did I Get Here?    60

**Searching for Peter Palagi: The Search for Purpose**    **75**

The Meeting Begins    113

*Epilogue*    *123*

*Author's Reflections*    *135*

*About the Author, Alejandro Arteaga*    *139*

# INTRODUCTION

A famous, well-known person is a celebrity. There is usually a certain amount of fascination with celebrity status, and people are interested in everything about them. Some celebrities are more famous than others, and the fascination with the most famous ones is on a much higher scale.

A well-known business can also be considered a "celebrity business," attracting a similar level of interest and curiosity about its operations and history. In my opinion, Palagis Ice Cream Company falls into that category—at least on a local level in the state of Rhode Island.

There are usually some obvious reasons why a person or a business becomes famous and reaches celebrity status. In the case of Palagis Ice Cream Company, there are several. One reason is the reach we have—on average, about five thousand people step up to one of the Palagis Ice Cream trucks daily during the season to get a treat. And it's not just a simple transaction. It is often a very special and joyful moment, a highlight of the day, especially for those who don't experience it regularly.

When we arrive at an event—whether it's a private party, an employee appreciation gathering, or one of the many occasions requesting our services—there is usually a mix of people from different backgrounds and walks of life. Many of these individuals don't see an ice cream truck often, making our presence a thrilling moment. People line up, conversations spark about the truck, and friendly banter creates a warm, happy atmosphere, almost as if the truck itself possesses a magical aura.

Almost without fail, someone starts with a story: "I remember when..." and goes on to share a childhood memory or a significant moment involving the ice cream truck—more specifically, a Palagis Ice Cream Truck. These stories might be from just a few weeks ago or stretch back 50 years. Some even mention Peter Palagi by name. One story leads to another, and soon, a whole conversation unfolds.

Another key reason for Palagis Ice Cream Company's celebrity status is its longevity. Founded in 1896, it remains in business 129 years later, serving four generations of Rhode Islanders—literally millions of people—creating unforgettable memories of childhood summers. I know firsthand about the deep appreciation for this business because I have run it for the past 25 years.

Whenever I meet someone and they learn that I'm in the ice cream business, they immediately smile—what I like to call "showing me their teeth." When they discover I'm associated with Palagis Ice Cream, their excitement multiplies as they are familiar with it and likely have their own cherished memories.

There aren't many businesses whose mere mention can evoke such joy. Just hearing the word "ice cream" brings happiness, but when it's paired with "Palagis Ice Cream" or "Peter Palagi," it becomes personal, transporting people back to a cherished childhood memory of a summer long ago.

Now, in 2025—129 years and counting—Palagis Ice Cream Company is still going strong. Through four generations and a few minor variations in its name over the years, it has endured, summer after summer, through some of the most significant events in American history—including some difficult times.

Some of these historical events include:

- **World War I** (1914–1918)

- **Black Tuesday** (1929), the stock market crash that triggered the Great Depression, which lasted about a decade

- **World War II** (1939–1945), the deadliest and most destructive war in history

- **The bombing of Pearl Harbor** (1941), which led the U.S. to formally enter World War II

- **The Civil Rights Movement** (1950s–1960s), a period marked by the assassinations of two American icons—John F. Kennedy in 1963 and Martin Luther King Jr. in 1968

- **The moon landing** (1969), when Neil Armstrong famously declared, "One small step for man, one giant leap for mankind"

- **September 11, 2001** (9/11), a tragedy most of us witnessed live on television

Through it all, Palagis Ice Cream Company remained, opening its doors summer after summer.

I'm going to go out on a limb here and call Palagis Ice Cream Company one of the most—if not the most—impactful businesses in the state of Rhode Island over the past 129 years, in terms of touching the most lives, creating joyful, lasting memories for generations. If you were fortunate enough to live in an area where a Palagis truck passed by daily, you were part of something special—something millions of Rhode Islanders have experienced over more than a century.

Peter Palagi became as American as apple pie—the best of American culture, at least on a local level.

After experiencing the curiosity and fascination surrounding this business, I realized that this story ought to be told—and who better to tell it than me? If anyone else told it, the past 25 years would be missing. Told by me, it will be complete. After all, perhaps it was my destiny to reach this point and share this story.

This is my attempt, and I hope it is interesting, captivating, and entertaining enough for people to enjoy and appreciate.

# SEARCHING FOR
# PETER PALAGI

# 1

# THE EARLY DAYS

## THE IMMIGRANT EXPERIENCE

Pietro Palagi emigrated from Italy to the USA in 1896. Immigrants arrived in this great new land called America with high hopes—a place with unlimited opportunities and possibilities. He settled in Pawtucket, Rhode Island.

Like all immigrant stories, upon arrival, they had to find work to support themselves and establish a way to make a living. They also shared common traits, among them a willingness to work as hard as necessary to succeed. The initial goal was simply to make their way, but beyond that was the realization that it would be a shame not to take full advantage of the extraordinary opportunities available in this new land. Pietro was no different. He knew success would only come with great discipline, dedication, and sacrifice.

Having an entrepreneurial mindset, as many immigrants did at the time, Pietro tried his hand at several different businesses, such as selling fruits and vegetables, as well as working in the ice business. The ice business fizzled, and he saw no real opportunity in it. He continued selling fruits and vegetables and eventually added popsicles to his inventory when he came across an icebox and used dry ice to keep them frozen.

He quickly realized there was a strong demand for his ice popsicles, especially when the weather turned nice.

Being in this new land, Pietro Palagi adopted his American name and became known as Peter Palagi. He was very involved in his community, helping new Italian immigrants settle in their new country. He provided jobs when he could and even helped some people keep their homes by assisting with mortgage payments, particularly during the difficult times of the Great Depression. Always willing to lend a hand to a fellow Italian, Peter was undoubtedly a well-respected leader in the community and a hardworking, entrepreneurial businessman.

## THE ICE CREAM WAGONS
## (THE BEGINNINGS OF THE ICE CREAM TRUCK)

As Peter noticed the demand for his popsicles, he wanted to expand that part of his business. He obtained another icebox and built a cart to easily transport it to different locations. He started taking the cart to downtown Pawtucket, just down the street from his house on Main Street, where he would sell fruits and vegetables. Downtown was bustling with activity from late morning to early afternoon, but he soon realized that foot traffic there was limited to only a portion of the day. Knowing there was strong demand for his products, he sought other locations that would be busy at different times of the day.

Peter eventually loaded the icebox onto a wagon pulled by a horse and moved from the downtown location, which was busy in the afternoon, to areas where more people gathered in the evenings. As this became a daily routine, Peter became known as the ice cream man. People began to recognize his route and requested that he stop by their homes on his way from one location to another or on his way home at the end of the day.

It didn't take long for Peter to realize he was onto something. By constantly being on the move, he could reach more people and offer them special frozen treats. As word spread about his service, he became overwhelmed with requests for home visits. To maximize his opportunity, he needed to cover more ground within the same hours of the day. So, Peter built another ice cream wagon, acquired another icebox, and hired people to run additional wagons while still operating his own. He added a few more product options and officially named his business Peter Palagi Ice Cream, which was displayed on all the wagons. This marked the beginning of the ice cream wagon, which would eventually lead to the invention of the ice cream truck. Through his work and innovations, Peter would become known as "the father of the ice cream truck."

## ICE CREAM TRUCKS—THE MODEL A FORDS

After about three decades in business and considering its growth, it was time to transition from horse-drawn wagons to automobiles, which were becoming more popular and more practical. Automobiles offered an opportunity to cover more ground and expand their reach. In 1931, they started with a couple of Model A Fords.

Peter became a living legend, and part of that legend was the fleet of Model A Ford ice cream trucks they used after upgrading from horse-drawn wagons. There were six of these trucks, each bearing the name "Peter Palagi Ice Cream," making Peter a familiar presence everywhere. Whoever drove these trucks was often called "Peter," and they would even answer to that name. The mere sight of one of these trucks or

*Fleet of Ford Model As, 47 Water Street.*

the mention of the name Peter Palagi takes people back to a summer long ago and cherished childhood memories.

One of the original 1931 Model A Ford ice cream trucks remains at the company headquarters on 55 Bacon Street. It has been sitting idle inside the building for 40 years and is currently in the process of being restored. This is a special truck.

In the antique car and truck world, every vehicle has a story and a history—but none with a history quite like "The Peter Palagi Model A Ford Ice Cream Truck." A fleet of six Model A Ford Peter Palagi Ice Cream Trucks worked the streets of Pawtucket and surrounding communities for approximately 50 years. One could estimate that the number of people who stepped up to buy ice cream from one of these trucks could be anywhere from at least a million to a few million. I challenge anyone to come up with a vehicle story that can match that impact—or even come close to it.

*Ford Motor Company*

THE AMERICAN ROAD
DEARBORN, MICHIGAN

July 6, 1960

Mr. Peter P. Palagi
Vice President
Palagi's Ice Cream Company
47 Water Street
Pawtucket, Rhode Island

Dear Mr. Palagi:

Thank you very much for sending the photograph of your old Ford trucks. It is one of the nicest fleets of its kind that we have seen in a long time.

I am holding the picture aside on the possibility we can use it in the FORD TIMES at some later date. I know that our readers will be very much interested and pleased.

Sincerely yours,

Robert Martin Hodesh
Associate Editor
FORD TIMES

RMH/z

*Ford Motor Company*
THE AMERICAN ROAD
DEARBORN, MICHIGAN

Mr. Peter P. Palagi
Vice President
Palagi's Ice Cream Company
47 Water Street
Pawtucket, Rhode Island

## LOCATIONS

A history of Palagi Ice Cream's locations:
- **12 Main Street** –

- **47 Water Street** –

- **55 Bacon Street** – In 1966, the company purchased land at this location but faced court battles from neighbors opposing their right to build there. These legal battles lasted from 1967 to 1969. Today, the company remains at this location—58 years later.

# 2

# THE ROLE OF
# THE FAMILY

As Peter was building his business, he was also raising a family. He married Severina Finucci in 1899, and
together they had 11 children:

- Mariana Palagi Martini
- Eduard
- Emma Palagi Farley
- Philip
- Henry
- Lola Palagi
- Peter Palagi Jr.
- Anna Palagi
- Emerica Palagi
- Ella Palagi
- Mathilde (Tilly)

Sundays were family days when they would gather at
Peter's house, spend the day together, and share a meal.

Peter Jr. was the youngest son, and his name would
become synonymous with "the ice cream man." The company

survived three generations of the Palagi family. From its start in 1896, Peter Sr. owned and ran the company until the 1940s, when his four sons—Eduard, Henry, Philip, and Peter Jr.—took over. Eduard passed away in 1956, and Henry retired in the late 1950s, leaving Peter Jr. and Philip to run the business through the second generation.

## PETER JR. & PHILIP

When I started working at Palagi Ice Cream, Peter Jr. was still around. Though retired, he was at the shop every day, helping his son Donald run the company—even though he had been retired for at least a dozen years. He was in his late seventies at the time. His "no excuses, the show must go on" mentality was an inspiration to everyone, as he was totally committed to helping his son keep the business going despite daily challenges. He was also mechanically inclined and always fixing or improving something.

*Peter and his brother Philip.*

*Donald and Uncle Philip.*

*Address: 129 Main Street.*

*Philip, 1968.*

*Donald and his father, Peter.*

Many people who knew him, especially those who remembered him as their ice cream man, would recall how much they liked him and how kind he was. He was a people pleaser.

Peter had many stories to tell, and one that stands out the most is about when he first started peddling ice cream. As they referred to selling back in the day, he was nine years old when his father told him to just get on the wagon and not to worry about the route—the horse knew the way. Along the route, there were places where the horse would stop for a break and to drink some water.

Peter would also talk about his favorite horse, "Good old Tom," as he would refer to him. They had a few horses, and he would tell us about the times they had a few runaways.

You could hear in his voice and see the passion he had for peddling ice cream and making people happy when he told his stories. At times, you could see Peter in deep thought while reminiscing about the past. He would often say how he wished he was still peddling ice cream.

Peter ran the company with his brother, Philip, for about 30 years, having worked in the business together for a lifetime, starting from an early age.

In the running of the company, Peter was the handy, "able-to-fix-everything" man, while Philip had a reputation as quite the salesman. Great salespeople all have one thing in common—they work long hours. That is exactly what Philip did. He worked long hours, along with demonstrating the other qualities that make one a good salesperson—or good at anything, really—a positive attitude, consistency, and discipline.

One of the stories about Philip that has stuck with me is about how, when some of the other peddlers got a late start—perhaps due to a rainy or cloudy day—they would gather at a local diner for breakfast. While they were still eating, Philip would drive by in his ice cream truck, ring the bell, and tell them they were falling behind. He would let them know how much ice cream he had already sold while they were still

*Peter on one of his regular visits*
*and me, Alejandro (Alex).*

Ice cream maker-vendor Don Palagi, between old and new

## ...we all still scream for Palagi's

having breakfast. That was the discipline and dedication he brought with him every day.

In 1976, Peter's son, Donald, bought the company from his father and his Uncle Philip, passing on the family business to the third generation.

Donald returned to the family business after attending the University of Rhode Island (URI), where he studied engineering and business. At the time, he left a career in business management to come back to the family business. With the transition to a third-generation family member, the company's name changed from Peter Palagi Ice Cream to Palagi's Ice Cream Company. Donald ran the company until its 100th anniversary in 1996.

After that milestone, Donald began contemplating retirement, and in 1998, he sold the company to Alejandro (Alex) Arteaga. The company changed hands to a fourth generation, but this time, the new owner was not a family member. Alex had been working with the company for the previous 10 years as one of the on-street vendors—an ice cream man—serving the city of Central Falls and the Pawtucket/Lincoln Fairlawn area.

Alex was also an immigrant, having come to the U.S. from his native Colombia in 1976 at the age of nine, settling in Cumberland, Rhode Island, with his family. With this new change in ownership, the company's name changed once again. Palagi's Ice Cream Company became simply Palagis Ice Cream. The only barely noticeable change was the removal of the apostrophe in "Palagi's," making it just "Palagis Ice Cream."

The story of Palagis Ice Cream continues—a new chapter in the life of this historic and beloved company.

# 3

# NEW OWNERSHIP–A NEW CHAPTER IN THE HISTORY OF PALAGIS ICE CREAM COMPANY, A NEW GENERATION & 4TH GENERATION OF COMPANY OWNERSHIP

## MY STORY

The year was 1999, the first year of new ownership for this Pawtucket, Rhode Island-based company, which had been around for over a century and had become an institution. The fourth generation took over, but for the first time, the new owner was not a family member.

The new owner was Alejandro (Alex) Arteaga. Alex had been working with the company for the previous ten years, running a truck route in Central Falls and the Fairlawn section of Pawtucket/Lincoln.

At the time of the new ownership in 1999, the company had eight trucks. In the next four years, the fleet would double from eight to sixteen trucks. While the opportunity was

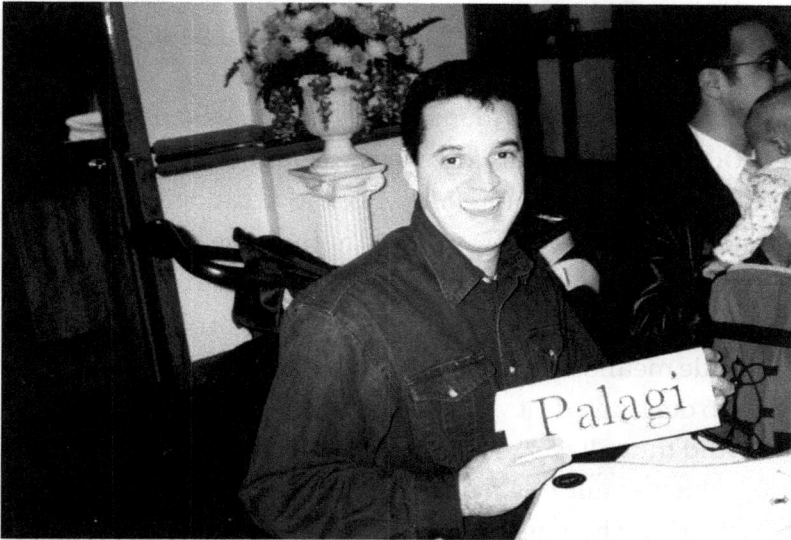

*Pawtucket Hall of Fame induction for Peter Palagi.*

exciting, it was certainly an extraordinary challenge to maintain and grow at the same time. As Albert Einstein once said, "In the middle of every difficulty lies opportunity." Being the positive person that I am, I saw this as an opportunity for personal growth and a chance to strengthen my resolve.

Difficult times often spark creativity and begin the problem-solving process, leading to new ways of doing things that might never have been thought of without the challenges that arose

## MBAs

I came into the business with an MBA. An MBA, or Master of Business Administration, is typically earned after two years of schooling following a bachelor's degree, which takes about four years to complete. So, in total, it takes about six years to obtain an MBA. However, I didn't get one of those six-year degrees. I got a different kind of MBA—the kind that's

earned through life's experiences, which teach you the importance of a good attitude.

Dave Thomas, the founder of Wendy's, who passed away
in 2002, talks about his MBA in one of his books, *Dave's Way*.
Dave's MBA stands for "Mop Bucket Attitude," which may
sometimes be even more important than the other MBA that
requires six years of schooling. If you have that six-year MBA
but a bad attitude, you might not get very far. A Mop Bucket
Attitude means the willingness to do whatever it takes to get
the job done and do it well. It's the belief that no job is beneath
you and that all work is honorable. A Mop Bucket Attitude is
also about quality—good enough is not good enough.

As Dave Thomas said, "I believe that as a CEO, one ought
to lead by example. If a leader is not willing to do something
himself, then he should not ask his employees to do it. A leader
should be the biggest team player, coach, and cheerleader, let-
ting everyone know that we're all in this together."

I have been fortunate to have people around me who
proudly displayed their MBAs (Mop Bucket Attitudes) on a
daily basis, especially during tough times. One person who
stands out is Rod, who helped me run the company for 20
years. Rod was always willing to do whatever needed to
be done—and then some. Though he was not a mechanic,
it wasn't unusual to see him changing a tire or doing some
mechanical work to get a truck running. He wore many hats.
Everything he did was always with a good attitude, for the
good of the team. He was a true team player.

With Rod by my side, I had the confidence to believe we
could make it all work and that everything would be okay.

Then there's the story of Manuel. I could dedicate a whole
chapter to Manuel, but this humble, quiet man would not
appreciate that. So I'll just tell you a little about him, as he is
a big part of this story. Manuel also has an MBA.

*Manuel in his lemonade station.*

The year was 2001, and Manuel had just arrived from the Dominican Republic. Manuel's stepson, who was working with us at the time driving an ice cream truck, told us that his stepfather had just arrived from the Dominican Republic and asked if we would mind if he came by and helped out

*Manuel, always finding something to do, often doing things we didn't even know needed doing*

by washing some of the drivers' trucks since he wasn't doing anything. Whoever wanted their truck washed could give him a couple of dollars; he was okay with that. Manuel said it would be better than staying home doing nothing. We said, "Sure, no problem." Manuel was about 63 years old at the time.

At that time, I was still on the road driving an ice cream truck and doing a route. I thought it was pointless to have my truck washed since I washed my own truck every day. I had my routine, and it worked for me.

Manuel showed up every day—seven days a week—to take care of those who had asked him to wash their trucks. This was his big responsibility. He was an early riser and would get there around 6 a.m. after walking about a mile from his house. He didn't like waiting around doing nothing, so he always seemed to find something to do, keeping himself busy by picking up trash, sweeping, helping people with their orders, etc... etc...etc. He became very useful to everyone, never asking for money or even for a regular job. He simply helped out and was useful, doing things we didn't even realize needed doing.

That year, I built Peter Palagi's Playground. As part of that project, I had a 250- to 300-foot wooden fence installed at the far side of the property. I wanted to protect the fence and decided to have it stained—or maybe even do it myself. I bought a five-gallon bucket of stain. As I saw Manuel hanging around and noticing his willingness to help out, I asked him one day if he wanted to help me with the fence. I told him there was no hurry and we could do a little each day. That same day, I had to go out and run some errands, but when I returned, I saw something that I'll never forget. Manuel had already begun working on the fence—not only had he begun, he was over halfway done. What I thought would take a few days, or even a week, Manuel turned into a few hours of work. At that moment, I realized this man was no ordinary man.

Seeing his willingness to help out and always keeping himself busy, we started asking him to do more. Since we knew he was an early riser, we asked him if he wanted to come in earlier—at 4:30 a.m.—and help with the making of the lemonade and pouring it into the trucks. We offered him that job, and he created his own role with his extraordinary attitude.

The next day, he was there before Rod, who had been making the lemonade. Rod, being the proud man he was, wanted to be there before Manuel, but Manuel would typically beat him as Rod had an hour-long commute. Manuel quickly learned how to make the lemonade, and he's been making it ever since.

If you've bought frozen lemonade from one of our trucks from 2002 to 2024, chances are Manuel made that lemonade. For those of you old enough to remember the Dunkin' Donuts commercial with Fred, who got up early every day with the slogan "Time to make the donuts," well, Manuel was our version of Fred—except instead of donuts, it was lemonade. "Time to make the lemonade" every day, without fail, no excuses. He had an extraordinary sense of responsibility. If Manuel committed to something, you could rest assured it was as good as done.

Now it is 2025, and Manuel is 87 years old. We are just a few months away from yet another ice cream season, and Manuel is planning on coming back to help out. Besides making lemonade, Manuel washes trucks, checks oil, changes tires, and is my alarm clock when I'm running late. If I am behind, I would get a call from him. He is also the motor and the computer of Palagis Ice Cream Company. When I say "the computer," I mean Manuel is the go-to guy when we forget something that happened the previous week, month, or even years ago. If I need to ask about something, I ask Manuel, and chances are high that he'll remember, like a computer storing all that information. He has the best memory of any of us, even though he's the oldest by far. As my mother would say, "Amazing." Manuel has his MBA, but his MBA is special—he's still with us and still doing it all.

Manuel never learned to read, as he only attended first grade. Don't let that fool you. I don't know how IQ is measured, especially when the person being tested cannot read, but I wouldn't be surprised if his number came up at the top of the charts for all the people working with us. He couldn't read, but don't try to fool him about his numbers—he knows his numbers. There are also signs of a photographic memory. He's the go-to guy when we forget things.

Another totally committed person on the team, making sure everything got done and that everything needing attention received it, was Geo (Geovanni). Geo also started with us by just coming around to help fix little things, and like Manuel, he created his own job. He became part mechanic, part keeper of everything neat and accounted for, and the go-to guy for anything miscellaneous. About three years ago, he had shoulder surgery, and his body could no longer handle that kind of work. We can always count on him when we need an extra hand or have questions about truck parts or advice on diagnostics of truck problems. He still comes around and would never let you down.

Then there's Gustavo, who made sure that everything that needed fixing got fixed. Gustavo is a master of all trades: plumbing, electrical, carpentry, building, and idea generation. Again, he was totally committed to doing whatever needed doing, and no job was beneath him, which is one of the great traits of an MBA. He also runs an ice cream truck route.

What a treasure to have someone like that around! Yes,

Gustavo was a treasure to have, but actually, they all were, each for their own skills and abilities. But more importantly, they were valued for their total dedication, commitment, and great attitudes.

Everyone on the team needs to be appreciated for their contributions—both the great and the small. Great appreciation is due to the drivers, the ice cream men (and sometimes ice cream ladies) who go on the road and bring ice cream treats to different cities and towns across the state of Rhode Island on a daily basis. These are disciplined, hard-working individuals running their own businesses and working seven days a week. These drivers complete Team Palagis. We've been very fortunate to have such a dedicated group of people working with us. More than 80% of the drivers have been with us for over a dozen years, and most for even longer.

## PETER PALAGI'S PLAYGROUND (2001)

In 2001, I took on a project that, looking back now, was premature in terms of timing. I was just starting to figure things out and trying to get a handle on everything, especially finances, as I was heavily mortgaged at the time. This new project would require that I get additional funding to make it happen. At the same time, we also began the process of renewing the fleet. I wrote a business plan and managed to get a loan not only for two new trucks but also for my project.

The project was the building of Peter Palagi's Playground and Ice Cream Shack, overlooking McCoy Stadium. When it was completed, it was a beautiful playground with perfectly manicured grass, a rock pond with a waterfall, Koi fish, and a white picket fence—almost like a dream. It was only open for three years, as it didn't work out as I had hoped. One of the main reasons was the liability of owning a playground and

*Peter Palagis Playground opening day.*

# Pawtucket's Peter Palagi Playground Ribbon Cutting

The family tradition continued at the opening of the Peter Palagi Playground on Bacon Street in Pawtucket. First there was Peter Palagi, Jr. and his son Donald joining in the festivities. Then there was Alex Arteaga, current owner of the business, and his sister and brother-in-law and lots of family members joining in the celebration.

Alex was telling Mayor Jim Doyle and My Backyard that Peter age 93 stops in each morning at the shop to make sure things are going along o.k. One of Alex's on going projects, now that the playground is done is restoring one of the original Palagi ice-cream trucks. Michael, Mayor Doyle and I got an up-front and personal view of the restoration project.

Rod Florez is the manager of the business and guardian of the playground. He said the playground will be an asset to the neighborhood. He is sure everyone will respect the property.

Maria Florez was mistress of ceremonies and chief greeter for the grand opening. She was very proud of the park and pleased at the community turnout.

Alex is a detail guy. He was checking on the gold fish in the ponds and making certain each child got a turn in the playground. These are good people doing a good thing. Check it out. We wish them well.

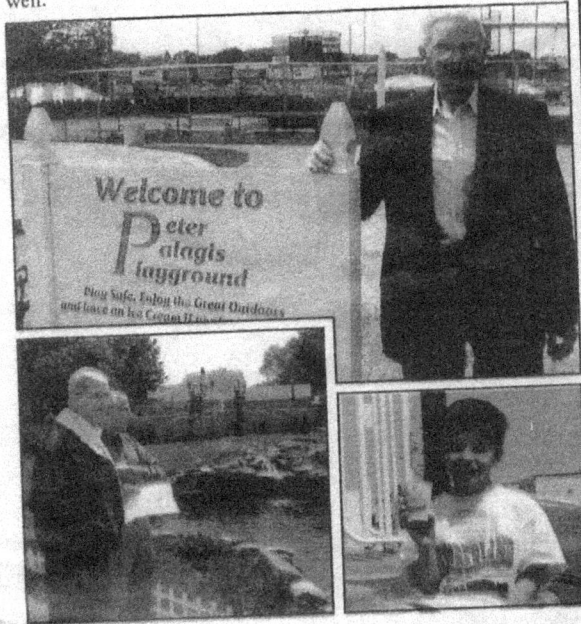

Welcome to Peter Palagis Playground

You Can Afford To Advertise In My Bacl

Monday, May 19, 2003

# LOCAL/OBITUARIES

# Peter Palagi Playground opens

■ Project honors the founder of famous local ice-cream company

**By TIM GRACE**
Times staff reporter

PAWTUCKET — For more than a century, Peter Palagi's signature ice cream trucks have been making their way to parks across the city.

After Sunday's grand opening of the Peter Palagi Playground, a park has finally come to the trucks.

Hundreds — including 93-year-old Peter Palagi Jr., the son of the company's founder — gathered at Palagi Ice Cream headquarters on Bacon Street, next door to the McCoy Stadium annex, for the afternoon ribbon-cutting ceremony.

Dozens of children were among the first to try the swings, slides and jungle gym, while their parents soaked up the late-spring sun on wrought-iron park benches and at picnic tables, enjoying complimentary cones and frozen lemonade.

Alex Arteaga, the 36-year-old owner of the Palagi company and a Palagi customer since the days of his youth in Central Falls, said he's been working on the park project for the last five years, suffering a few setbacks and design changes along the way.

As built, the park is comprised of a large, rolled-out lawn intersected by a system of curving, crushed gravel foot paths. Purple dinosaur slides, swings, plastic tunnels and monkey bars are set in three play areas and Palagi's Ice Cream Shack sits to one side, ready to serve.

"Anything that bears the name of Peter Palagi must have something to do with fun and happiness," Arteaga said, explaining to the crowd why he's put so much effort

JOE ANGELL/For The Times

Josh Mimasian, 5, right, and Nick Crawley, 4, both of Pawtucket, check out the new swings, slides and jungle gym at Sunday's grand opening of the Peter Palagi Playground.

into maintaining and expanding the local landmark business.

"It's easy to open a business in this country, but to keep it going and to make it profitable is quite a challenge," he said. "To keep it going for 100 years, in my mind, is a monumental achievement."

"Mr. Palagi brought a lot of happiness to a lot of people for many, many years," Arteaga's sister, Maria Florez, said during the event.

Donald Palagi, Peter's son, attended the opening with his father. He remembered his uncles, Eddie Philip and Henry Palagi, "putting their lives and souls into this business along with my father.

"They're in a better place now, but they're probably still out ringing that bell and looking for kids."

The park will be open from 11:30 a.m. to 9 p.m., 10 p.m. in July and August, according to Arteaga. Off-street parking is available in the lot adjacent to the Palagi garage.

---

the risks associated with that. Regardless of how it worked out, I was left with a bigger mountain of debt than the one I started with.

I only knew one option: I borrowed the money, I pay the money. As you can imagine, the struggle to get through, make a living, pay down the debt, and make enough to further invest in the business to move it forward, was tough.

Whenever I talk about those days, I often describe them as the time when I was young, full of energy and ambitious—really kind of poking fun at myself, saying I wanted to do too much too soon. Looking back now, I could have used the word "naive." I had a lot to learn.

Well, here we are, twenty-something years later, and I'm proud to say I never missed a payment, neither in the business nor in my own personal life with my own bills. On top of that, we were able to grow. I often use the quote, "That which does not kill you will only make you stronger," credited to the German philosopher Friedrich Nietzsche. I strongly believe in that. The struggle is a positive thing, even though it may not feel good at the time. It forces you to learn how to navigate through the rough waters to get to the other side. You then own the lessons you've been forced to learn from those experiences.

## RUNNING A BUSINESS IS NOT ALL SUNSHINE AND ROSES

Running a business is not all sunshine and roses. You take on an extraordinary obligation and responsibility, where you learn to live in a world with no excuses. You must have a "the show must go on" mentality. In fact, the reason you got the opportunity in the first place was that you had already shown that this is the world you've been living in for some time.

Without a doubt, there are many times of uncertainty when you feel that the weight of the world is on your shoulders. At times, you wonder if all this heavy lifting, stress, obligation, and responsibility are really worth it—not to mention the great commitment of time required to make it all work. Six months, 26 weeks, seven days a week, 80-plus-hour weeks, give or take.

Donald Palagi, Peter Palagi Jr.'s son, sold the business to me and helped me with a portion of the financing. I appreciated Donald for doing that, but at the same time, I felt pretty proud of myself, as I felt I had earned that trust and respect by displaying my work ethic, discipline, and "no excuses" attitude. Donald had total faith in me, knowing that I would somehow find a way and make it all work.

I visited Donald's insurance agent at the time, and he laughed and made a comment: "So, you're the last man on the totem pole." I asked him what he meant. He said, "Well, you're the last man to get paid—if you can get paid at all." I didn't realize it at the time how true that was.

You often hear stories of people who have been in business for a long time. They talk about the early days and make comments such as, "I couldn't take a pay for the first few years." After getting through the lean beginnings, you can sympathize with that comment, and you know how true it is, especially if you've ever tried your hand at starting a business.

There is a saying, "Running a business is not for the faint of heart. It's for the brave, the patient, and the persistent. It's for the overcomer" (anonymous). Here I was with my great new opportunity, and now realizing that I was the last man on the totem pole—thanks to my new insurance agent who let me in on that little secret.

As people see lines of people buying your products, their first thought—and often their only thought—is that you're getting rich. They don't realize that this business you run has quite an appetite and needs to be fed to keep it going. The bigger the business, the bigger the appetite. Sometimes you fall behind on paying bills, not for lack of money, but more for lack of time to sit down and make payments. So money accumulates, and for a brief time, you think you're doing pretty well. Then you get a chance to catch up and pay some bills. Then reality sets in, and there's barely enough money in the account to pay for everything. This almost sounds like mismanagement, but you're working as hard as you can and being as conservative as you can, eventually realizing how much there is still to learn to make it all work.

I went to college for one year, then I started working, and I believe that I got a much better education than most—an education that was the result of the struggle, patience, and confidence to get through to the other side.

Stubbornness is not always a good thing, but in my case, I was always glad that I was stubborn and didn't allow myself to be easily defeated, no matter how tough the situation became. Determination and a strong sense of conviction were my stubbornness, in a good way, that got me through.

# 4

# SOME CHALLENGING TIMES–
# THE PLIGHT OF SMALL
# BUSINESS

The life of a business is like the life of a person—there are lots of ups and downs, hopes and dreams to work toward, and a lot of effort and time needed to realize those goals. Sometimes things work out wonderfully, and sometimes they just don't.

During the life of that business, you work really hard and try to be as proactive as you can to avoid potential problems that would be difficult to overcome. Problems are energy-draining and morale-downers. At times, an unexpected situation arises out of nowhere—the opponent within—and a battle ensues. The battle between the opponent within, which is the challenge that appears unexpectedly out of the blue, and you—your patience, will, and determination to push through and overcome the challenge without being defeated by it.

When you reflect on your time at the helm of that business, the most memorable moments are those uncertain and difficult times when you almost lost your grip and were on the verge of being knocked out by the challenge. It's in these moments, when you were on the verge of sinking but managed to stay afloat, that you were truly defined. These are the moments that best define you and your tenure as the captain of the ship.

## FINDING THE RIGHT PEOPLE TO WORK

Common sense tells us that in order to build a business, you need to do more work, and in order to do more work, you need to find more people to help out. As is the case with most businesses, finding people to work is not necessarily difficult, but finding the right people for your particular situation is not easy. As many of you know, we sell ice cream, and we sell it from our Palagis Ice Cream Trucks, which are driven by self-employed individuals running their own seasonal ice cream businesses.

Anyone who has ever run a seasonal business—or knows anything about one—will tell you how hard it is to make it. One of the key ingredients is to work as much as you can, as time and weather allow. That being said, working seven days a week is part of the formula that gives you a chance at success.

Whenever we advertise for a job looking for people to run these businesses, we always use the phrase, "Must be willing and able to work seven days a week, 10- to 12-hour days." We quickly found that some people were willing but not able, while others were able but not willing. Some people simply could not commit due to life circumstances—family or other obligations that come with a normal life. Others were able to do it but not willing to make the sacrifice of giving up a normal life.

So, our number one challenge right off the bat was finding people who were both willing and able to make that commitment responsibly. They were few and far between. You'd have to try twenty different people to maybe find one good candidate who had a shot at making it.

## CHALLENGING TIMES: HURRICANE IRENE (2011)

Another particularly challenging time that stands out in my memory happened in late August 2011. We live in the age of Google, where if you're curious about something, you just ask Google. I did exactly that—I asked, "What happened in late August 2011?" The answer came right up. Amazing, as my mom would say. It really is incredible that we live in a time where we can access any information we're curious about simply by speaking into a small square device we all carry in our pockets—our cell phones—which 98% of Americans have. Truly amazing, my mother was right.

Oops! Sorry, I took a detour and went off on a tangent. Now, back to the topic at hand—what happened in late August 2011?

In late August 2011, New England was hit by Hurricane Irene, leaving behind devastation and widespread power outages. When you're in the ice cream business and the electricity goes out, it's never good news.

I don't recall exactly how much inventory we had at the time, but between our walk-in freezer and all the freezers inside the trucks, we must have had somewhere between $30,000 and $40,000 worth of ice cream. *What to do... what to do... what to do?* Well, all hope was not lost. Thankfully, there was no real damage to the property, and no one was hurt. From that standpoint, we were in good shape. But with no electricity—and about $40,000 worth of ice cream in danger of melting within a day or two—we were in a concerning situation, to say the least. Especially in a seasonal business, where time is limited.

With a "The show must go on" mentality, we began figuring out how to get through this and, if at all possible, stay open rather than be forced to close. Not knowing whether the power outage would last a day, two days, or even longer, we needed to come up with a plan to protect our inventory—both in the walk-in freezer and inside the trucks.

As is common during weather emergencies, neighbors were outside assessing the damage. We soon realized that the power outages were scattered—some houses had electricity while others did not. We had at least 24 to 36 hours before the ice cream inside the walk-in freezer would start to melt, so our first priority was to figure out what to do with the trucks. We instructed all drivers to see if they could find someone they knew who still had electricity and ask if they could park their truck there overnight and plug in the freezer.

While that search was underway, we also had to figure out what to do with the inventory in the walk-in freezer. We contacted our ice cream supplier and asked if they had a refrigerated delivery truck we could use to store our ice cream. Fortunately, they were able to provide one.

We also found a garage about half a mile down the street that still had power. They were in the car detailing business, and we convinced the owner to let us park a few trucks there overnight and plug them in. Not knowing if this power outage would last a day or much longer, we had made the necessary adjustments to at least save our inventory. Things were starting to fall into place. If the emergency lasted longer than a couple of days, we could potentially keep going—but not without our famous frozen lemonade, which is our number-one-selling product and what truly keeps us in business.

Still maintaining our "The show must go on" mentality,

we brainstormed ways to make it all work. We asked the car detailing garage owner if we could bring one of our lemonade machines there, set it up, and make lemonade. He agreed—all in the spirit of helping us through this emergency.

Easier said than done. The batch freezer lemonade machine weighs about 5,000 pounds and required an electrical upgrade in that building to operate. We didn't know how long the power outage would last, but I've always had a "go, go, go" mentality—push forward until you can't go anymore or until something stops you. So, the thought was: *Let's do it. Let's not wait and see.*

We moved forward with the electrical upgrade—no small task—transported the 5,000-pound batch freezer, and set everything up in just a couple of days. The last piece of the puzzle was in place, allowing us to continue producing our famous frozen lemonade.

We were ready to proceed with business as usual—under highly unusual circumstances. At least for a day, two, seven, or beyond, if necessary. At the time, we had 20 trucks running, and each of those trucks was essentially its own separate business. Despite losing power due to a powerful storm, we made the necessary adjustments to keep those 20 businesses open, as well as our headquarters, all within just a couple of days.

Every evening, we made lemonade at the garage, transported it back to headquarters, and loaded it onto the trucks for the following day. We did this in total darkness every night for a full week while the power was out. In the mornings, we made more lemonade—but with only one machine, when we usually ran three.

The power was out for seven days, and we did not miss a beat. We did not close, and we did not lose any product.

What we accomplished that week was truly something

special—something to be proud of. Pulling that off was no small feat.

Had we been forced to close that week and lost all that product, it wouldn't have put us out of business, but it would have been a season of significant losses. In a seasonal business, **lost time is lost forever**—there's no way to make it up as the season dwindles and comes to an end.

## CHALLENGING TIMES: INSURANCE SCARE 2017

Another challenging aspect of running this business is the sensitive topic of insurance. As you know, this is the story of Palagis Ice Cream Company, whose main business is selling ice cream from ice cream trucks. And as you all know, you can't run a business without insurance, especially when your main business involves trucks. The more trucks you have, the more sensitive the issue becomes. We had built up the fleet to about 24 trucks but scaled back to a steady number of 22 trucks for some years, give or take. When it comes to insuring 22 company-owned trucks under the same policy, it gets complicated and expensive—especially when those trucks are ice cream trucks that spend the whole day on the road, driving around seven days a week.

Insurance companies often promote what they call bundling—offering a discount for purchasing different types of insurance from the same company. Here, we had a policy for 22 trucks—a nice bundle, for sure. Even though it wasn't different types of insurance, one would think that we would get a great deal and some discounts for insuring 22 trucks rather than just one.

The reality, however, was the opposite. The insurance company viewed us as having 22 trucks, meaning 22 drivers, and any one of those drivers could operate any of those trucks. If a single driver had a blemish on their driving record that increased their rate by $500, our policy would increase by $500 multiplied by 22 trucks—an $11,000 increase for the year. Another blemish? Another $11,000 hike, and so on. It was nearly impossible to have all 22 drivers maintain absolutely perfect records. There was always a red light violation, a stop sign infraction, a speeding ticket, a minor accident, or any number of incidents that could occur. As the years passed, insurance rates kept rising.

In 2012, we were approached by an insurance agent looking for new business. Given the situation of constantly rising prices, we kept an open mind and were willing to explore other options. We accepted his offer to research any new programs or alternative options for a business like ours. After a few days, he returned with a promising lead—a company that had just started a program for vending trucks. The quote he provided was far lower than what we had been paying, with much higher coverage. At the time, it was a no-brainer, and we switched coverage to that company.

We had a good five-year run with that company and the new policy. At the beginning of the 2017 season, however, we received a letter informing us that they would not be renewing our policy upon its expiration. Apparently, their experiment of insuring vending trucks at those rates had not worked out, and they were phasing it out.

Our season starts in late March or early April, weather permitting. Our renewal date for insurance was May 8th, which meant we could open for the season under the previous year's policy and rates until May 8th, at which point renewal would be necessary.

Knowing that our policy would not be renewed, we had to begin searching for new insurance. During this process, we were required to provide a five-year history—everything that had happened over that period. Naturally, as time passes, incidents accumulate. As mentioned earlier, it was almost impossible to maintain a completely clean record when our trucks were on the road for eight to ten hours a day, seven days a week, during the season. Something was bound to happen. While our record wasn't terrible, insurance companies viewed it differently. They aim to protect themselves, but as is often said about insurance, they look for every reason to charge you more and every reason to pay you less. They have the upper hand—they know we can't operate without insurance. Sometimes, it makes you wonder if they simply throw out high numbers with no real strategy. When you ask how they arrive at these numbers, no one really knows—they just input information into a system, and it spits out a figure.

The search for new insurance was quite an awakening. We began hearing the phrase "refuse to quote." After reaching out to multiple insurance agencies, the repeated response was "refuse to quote," making us realize that we might not find any company willing to take us on. We faced the very real possibility of having no choice but to close the business.

Obviously, we could not operate without insurance, so closure would have been our only option. It was a devastating thought—closing after more than 100 years in business and after all the hard work that had been put in. The idea that it would happen under my watch was particularly difficult to accept, especially when it was no fault of my own. History would record that the company closed under my leadership.

As reality set in, we considered the consequences: our livelihood, bankruptcy, foreclosure, and the need to find new employment to support our families. Sleepless nights followed.

Trying to get ahead of a potential crisis, I listed the property for sale as a worst-case scenario backup. If we had to close, selling the property would allow me to pay off the remaining balance and have some funds left to figure out the next steps. We even received a full-price offer.

At that moment, we had to decide the company's fate. Accepting the offer would likely mean the end of Palagis Ice Cream Company. Refusing the offer would mean paying the sales commission, as the real estate agent had done his job. It was a fork in the road, with two terrible options—more sleepless nights.

During this uncertain time, an insurance company finally gave us a quote. It was much higher than what we had previously paid, but at least it provided an alternative to closing down.

I refused the offer for the sale of the property, paid the commission, kept the property and the business intact, and continued operating. It was a huge relief—we had dodged that bullet.

## THE YEAR OF THE PANDEMIC: THE CHALLENGE OF THE PANDEMIC WHILE ALSO BUILDING *PALAGIS ICE CREAM SHACK*

The year was 2020—the infamous year of the pandemic. I remember watching the New Year's celebrations and seeing the number 2020, it looked perfectly balanced. It felt like it would be a great year... Then came the pandemic. What a time! A period of extraordinary uncertainty, leaving everyone wondering, "What now?"

Nearly 20 years prior, when I took on the project of creating Peter Palagis Playground and Ice Cream Shack, I would joke about being "young, full of energy, and ambitious." Now, 20 years later, I was not so young anymore—but still not so old, still full of energy, and still pretty ambitious. I embarked on a new project: building Palagis Ice Cream Shack. This time, there was no playground. Instead, I modified the existing building by creating a walk-up order window with an enclosed patio area with tables and eliminating the office space inside.

After the planning and permitting process, I began the physical work on December 28, 2019, just before New Year's. The first step was cutting a hole in the wall—there would be no turning back. The weather was beautiful for winter, with most days reaching the high 40s and low 50s, mostly sunny.

By January, news began circulating about a virus spreading on the other side of the world. The first U.S. case was reported on January 20, 2020. Then came March, and with it, the virus. By mid-March, it was declared a global pandemic, and businesses began shutting down. I was in the middle of my project and had to decide whether to continue investing money or hold off and see what happens.

As businesses closed, we were not allowed to open for the season, so I continued working on the Ice Cream Shack project, now with plenty of extra time.

It was a weird time—you would even wonder if money would lose all its value. Then they started closing down all the businesses. We were not allowed to open our business until the second week of May, losing out on about a month and a half of the season. When we were actually able to open for the season, while the pandemic was at its peak, I wasn't really sure what to expect. I thought it was going to be an extreme—either really, really bad for business or really good—one extreme or another and nothing in between. It was not an ordinary season, as what was happening was extraordinary in every sense.

Well, eventually, when we were able to go out to the streets and start selling ice cream, we were surprised in a good way. Just imagine—people had not been able to go out and were forced to stay home... then the ice cream truck shows up on your street. What an exciting moment! Just about everyone on that street would come out, as they had been stuck in their houses and unable to go anywhere else. The trucks that were able to go out would get large crowds on every street. The ice cream truck on your street became a sort of great escape from being locked inside and unable to go out, even if that escape was just to step outside, get some ice cream treats, maybe say hi to a neighbor, and get back in the house. What a great excuse to go outside.

The designated person who would come out often had a list of items for everyone in the house and sometimes two or three items per person, as they didn't know when they would get another chance to buy something in this most uncertain time. People were so appreciative of the ice cream truck visit that tips were at an all-time high. Every day was an extraordinary day... these were extraordinary times.

I was not on the road driving a truck; my work was all done at company headquarters, so I didn't experience the crowds on every street. But all the drivers reported the same experience all over the state, in different towns—a memorable time for sure.

At the end of the season, it was not the greatest in terms of sales, mainly due to the fact that we lost a month and a half of business. Additionally, many of the drivers were overseas and couldn't fly back, as most air travel was canceled until late June. The ice cream shack finally opened later that summer, sometime in mid-August.

The ice cream shack project was something I had always wanted to bring back. When I took on the Peter Palagi Playground project, I wrote a business plan in order to seek financing. With this new project, I also wrote a plan for what I was going to do, but it was not a business plan per se because it

# Nothing stops Palagis from bringing the goods

PAWTUCKET – Palagis ice cream mobile trucks have been ringing their bells along streets in local communities since 1896. Peter Palagi originally started selling ice cream from a freezer, which he eventually loaded onto a wagon pulled by a horse. That ice cream wagon made a daily route through the streets of Pawtucket.

We caught up with current owner Alex Arteaga, a member of the Palagi family, who's owned the company since 1998, to get the lowdown on how the Palagis drivers deliver their cold treats.

**How is business these days?**
With captive audiences staying at home during the pandemic, Arteaga says the company's drivers are regularly selling out of their popular items, all adding up to a banner year for Palagis even despite the lack of business from youth athletic events or other large gatherings. Continued limiting of large events this summer is expected to help keep neighborhood business strong.

**Is there an overarching strategy for ice cream truck drivers? Certain times down certain streets? Certain parts of town they know will never be profitable?**
There is no policy or best practices, as so much of good ice cream truck driving goes by feel and luck, says Arteaga. Particularly with regular Little Leagues and other sports not in session through spring and early summer, "there's no strategy" in the neighborhoods, he said. It's all about just going up and down streets in search of a friendly wave.

**What are some of the favorites?**
SpongeBob and Spider-Man popsicles are favorites among children, as are Two-Ball Screwballs and Snow Cones. For adults, the Big Dipper ice cream cone in multiple flavors and Cookies 'n Cream Screamers are two that are particularly popular.

**Can anyone drive an ice cream truck?**
Palagis is looking for personnel to fill positions as a driver/salesperson to drive trucks and sell ice cream in a Rhode Island community. They must be honest, reliable and responsible, at least 21 years old, have a valid driver's license, a good driving record, a clean background check, have good communication skills, be able to work long days, and be a self-starter. All are welcome to apply at Palagis Ice Cream Co., 55 Bacon St., Pawtucket, RI.

The Valley Breeze *article, summer 2020, the year of the pandemic.*

didn't include any numbers, nor did I need it to seek financing. It was more of a plan of action.

I believe that something written down encourages action to get it done. In this plan, there were three main points I wanted to emphasize. First, this project would be "an improvement and an enhancement to the neighborhood." Second, this project and the new space created would be "a gift to the community." And third, this would be a pivotal moment and a "game changer" in the history of this company. Now, we had a place where people would come to us, get to know us, and realize that there are some good people here with good intentions.

In 2022, we started the "Thursday Night Music Series"— live music for the community to enjoy, free of charge, as part of our gift to the community. That music series continued in 2023, and in 2024, in our third season, we doubled up, offering a second night of music on Sundays with a Latin flavor (Sabor Latino). I have always believed that we should all do what we can for our community—whatever benefits our community benefits all of us.

## INSURANCE SCARE #2 (2024)

After the insurance scare of 2017 that almost put us out of business, insurance rates kept rising year after year, mainly due to the sensitive nature of our business and the complexity of the policy. With so many moving parts—different drivers and possible small blemishes on some of their driving records—we always managed to make the necessary adjustments and make it work. Insurance rates were always an issue; year after year, they would go up. If one of the regular drivers—meaning someone who had been with us for a while and returned every year—had an accident or a moving violation, either with one of our trucks or their own car over the winter, that record would stay with us on our policy for three years, raising our rates. When the three-year period was over and cleared that particular driver's record, someone else would likely have an issue affecting their driving record. It was a losing battle.

It sounds like an easy fix—just hire people with clean driving records—but it wasn't that simple. These drivers were willing and able to work seven days a week and were committed to their business. It took a special kind of person to do that, and replacing them, thinking we could easily find someone else, was highly unlikely and nearly impossible.

Seven years after the 2017 insurance debacle, we entered the new season in 2024. As we began to add trucks to the policy, we started receiving letters from the insurance company regarding the new rates at renewal time, which was still May 8.

The first time I called in to add a couple of trucks at the end of March, they told me over the phone what the new rate would be at renewal time. The rate they gave me was $18,000-something per truck. That didn't make any sense to me—I thought it was a mistake—so I brushed it off and just added the two trucks for the time being, as we needed to start using them. The second time I called to make an addition, they told me the renewal rate again, but this time it had gone up to $19,000-something per truck.

The insurance agency that had handled our policy for many years and had been in business for over 75 years had just sold their business, and with it, all the accounts were transferred to the new company. So we had a new agent for our insurance.

Every time I called to add trucks, the renewal rate kept rising. The highest renewal quote I received was $24,000 per truck—WOW! That was more than a 400% increase in premiums from one year to the next. Do the math: $24,000 times 20 trucks equals $480,000 just to keep the business running. That was tough news to swallow, kind of like realizing mid-flight that something has gone terribly wrong and you're plummeting straight down. Well, maybe that's a little extreme. But at that moment, it felt like there was no other option but to crash and be forced to close. The difference between that scenario and this situation was that we had a little time to try to find a solution.

I still thought this had to be a mistake, but after hearing the same thing repeatedly, it became clear that these numbers were real. I began communicating with the new insurance agency, trying to get explanations, answers, and explore other options.

Here we go again—another insurance crisis. This time was different, though. We had the option to renew the policy, but at rates that were unsustainable. Renewal time was fast approaching.

Agreeing to those rates would have been like jumping off a ship in the middle of the ocean, hoping to swim to shore while knowing there was a 99.99% chance of drowning. It felt like financial suicide.

As I started coming to terms with the reality of the situation, stress and worry set in. Sleepless nights returned. As you can imagine, sleepless nights bring endless thoughts, desperate attempts to find a way through. It almost seemed illegal that an insurance company could do this. It felt like a bad joke—as if someone wanted us out of business and was doing this intentionally.

The insurance company held all the cards. They had the upper hand: either pay up or shut down. Committing to those rates would have undoubtedly put us out of business. Either way, the outcome seemed the same. Again, the same unsettling thoughts swirled in my mind: was this deliberate? It felt like a gun to our heads, forcing us to close.

None of it made sense to me, no matter how I looked at it. In trying to understand why the premiums had skyrocketed, they showed us a five-year loss run report detailing all incidents during that period. Yes, we had claims, and yes, they had paid out. But after adding up the total payouts, it was clear that even if they charged us the full amount for all claims, it would still be significantly less than what they were now demanding for just one season. No matter how I analyzed it, it didn't add up.

If they were charging us for everything that happened in the last five years, then what was the point of insurance? I understand high premiums based on a loss record, but this went beyond that. This was an attempt to recoup all their payouts in one season—and then some. I'm not sure what their numbers are, but I figured that for every claim filed, there are at least 10,000 customers paying premiums without filing a claim. The odds were heavily in their favor. Yet, I was driving myself crazy trying to make sense of it all.

The only way this would have made sense to me was if I had been an irresponsible policyholder—constantly hiring drivers with terrible records, DUIs, reckless driving, excessive speeding, and major at-fault accidents. If that had been the case, I could understand why they would want us to pay up or shut down. But that wasn't us.

In uncertain times like these, your mind runs wild with all sorts of scenarios. You try to find creative solutions, making sleep nearly impossible. That's what a crisis does to a person. It makes you feel like you're losing your mind.

For a while, I kept it all to myself, hoping to figure out a solution. I was the only one who knew. The very real possibility of having to close was back, and I didn't see a way out. It was like 2017 all over again. If the business closed, all the drivers and employees who depended on it would be out of work. And let's not forget the customers who relied on us for the special moments we helped create. The stress was overwhelming.

Eventually, I had to let the cat out of the bag. I called a meeting with all the drivers and told them the hard truth: there was a real chance we would have to close. Everyone loved what they did, and the mood turned somber. However, I assured them that my goal was to keep the business running through the season and then figure things out afterward. To do that, everyone would need to start paying more for truck expenses, including insurance. It was a difficult conversation, but at that moment, they seemed willing to do what it took to keep the business alive. After all, they weren't just employees; each of them was essentially running their own business.

More sleepless nights followed as I wondered if this plan would work. I knew there was a limit to how much I could charge before drivers started questioning if it was worth it. It was my best idea at the time, but I remained skeptical.

One idea that came to mind was finding an angel investor—someone with deep pockets who would see the value in Palagis Ice Cream and want to help. The inspiration for this came from a recent story in Pawtucket, where a billionaire tried to save McCoy Stadium from demolition to make way for a new high school. He thought the stadium was worth saving. He even floated a big dollar figure about how much he would be willing to spend. The story got a lot of attention at the time while the city leaders considered their options. If someone was willing to invest millions to save an empty stadium, surely they might see the worth in a 128-year-old, still-thriving business like ours.

In my opinion, the stadium was not worth saving. The

combination of the PawSox franchise and the stadium was worth saving, but the PawSox had already picked up and moved out of town to Worcester, leaving behind an empty stadium. My thinking was that if some people—or someone like this guy with a lot of money, an angel investor—thought the stadium was worth saving, then surely Palagis Ice Cream Company, with its 128-year history and lasting impact on this state, would be worth saving as well. That's where my idea of an angel investor came from.

Good idea or bad idea? I don't know. But it was an idea nevertheless—an idea born from the whirlwind of my wandering mind. All bets were on the table.

I usually come up with my best ideas after sleeping on them for a day or three. One night, I came up with another idea—a possible solution to this situation, a way to move forward and breathe new life into the business. I realized this was the best path forward, really the only way to save the company and stay in business.

I recognized that it wasn't in the company's best interest to own all these trucks and have them all under one insurance policy. Each driver should own their own truck and be responsible for their own insurance, maintenance, and upkeep. So I devised a plan to sell the trucks to the drivers. I put together a proposal that would be hard to refuse—offering very favorable terms and 100% financing. More than half of the drivers jumped at the opportunity and bought the trucks they were already driving. It was a great deal for them. After a couple of seasons, they would fully own their trucks. The money they had previously paid as a truck expense fee would now go toward paying off their own vehicle, like being forced to put money in the bank—a deal almost too good to be true.

Some drivers chose not to take advantage of the opportunity, each for their own personal reasons. Those who did move forward had to obtain their own insurance, register their trucks, and continue working as they had before—except now, they were fully responsible for their trucks, including insurance, maintenance, and repairs. The cost of individual insurance, compared to the company's group policy covering twenty trucks, came at an 80% to 90% discount—a very reasonable and workable expense. To put it bluntly, it was a hell of a deal.

All of this had to happen while we were still open for business—and in just two weeks. It was an incredibly tense time for me, trying to make it all work. Since not everyone participated in the program, I had to remove all the trucks from company ownership and insurance. That meant I needed to find new owners for the remaining trucks, and thankfully, a few people stepped in to help me with that.

Once the registrations were transferred over and most of the drivers became truck owners, something interesting started to happen. When you take ownership of something—like a house—you take pride in it. The same thing happened with these trucks. Just as a neighborhood of renters improves when it becomes a neighborhood of homeowners, these drivers started taking better care of their trucks.

They also began thinking about the future of their new businesses—considering passing them down to family members or someone they knew. They started fixing up their trucks and making them look good—responsibilities that had previously fallen on just one person: me, times twenty.

I am a firm believer that when one door closes, five windows open. When you're faced with a dead end, you're forced to consider options you never thought of before—and sometimes, you come out better on the other side. It reminds me of a quote from one of my favorite movies, *The Shawshank Redemption*. When Red tells the story of Andy's escape, he says, *"He (Andy) went through five hundred yards of poop and came out clean on the other side."*

Sometimes, extraordinary struggles serve as stepping-stones to a better place with firmer ground. Palagis Ice Cream Company just went through its toughest challenge, but we came out stronger and in a better position to move forward.

## 5

# THE MAGIC OF PETER PALAGI

Money can't buy you happiness, but you can buy ice cream, and it's essentially the same thing—especially when it comes from the ice cream truck.

When the subject of the ice cream truck comes up, people's memories go back to their childhood, and most have a story to tell. These stories are mostly centered on one common theme: the excitement of the moment upon the arrival of the ice cream truck. If you grew up in Rhode Island, the name that comes to mind when speaking of the ice cream truck is Palagis Ice Cream and/or Peter Palagi, the ice cream man.

Peter Palagi is the most famous ice cream man—at least on a local level—with good reason. He was the ice cream man in Pawtucket, Rhode Island, and surrounding communities for eighty years. The first forty years, it was Peter Palagi Senior, and for the next forty, it was his son, Peter Palagi Junior, who continued the tradition. Even though it was two different people spanning eighty years, they were both Peter Palagi, father and son.

With a fleet of six Ford Model A company trucks on the road for fifty years, all carrying the name "Peter Palagi Ice Cream," the brand's popularity multiplied, making him a legend. The name and the stories have been passed down from generation to generation, just like the Peter Palagi Ice Cream business, now in its fourth generation.

Just the mention of the name Peter Palagi takes people back to childhood memories and the great moments that were created because of what Peter did. Peter would show up day in and day out. The ice cream man coming—better yet, Peter Palagi showing up every day—was as much a sure thing as night turning into day... every day.

## THE MAGIC OF THE ICE CREAM TRUCK

Today, the arrival of the ice cream truck is just as exciting as it was one hundred years ago. Some people sing, some people dance, some tell stories, and it's almost unanimous that everybody's mood changes to happiness upon its arrival.

I will share a couple of stories about a memorable customer that I will never forget, which provides a glimpse of "the magic of the ice cream truck."

I had a young man who was a daily customer; if he was home, he was getting ice cream. His name was Sean, he had an older brother, Joseph. I had Sean as a customer for a few years. Guessing his age, he was a daily customer from five to eight years old. His brother Joseph was about two years older.

Sean's excitement level upon the arrival of the ice cream truck, on a scale of 1 to 10, was a solid and consistent 10—day in and day out. The big thrill of the day, every day, was just as exciting as the day before. Joseph, on the other hand, was more relaxed and calm. Even though he also liked ice cream, sometimes he didn't even want it.

One day, when I showed up, Sean ran out as he always did. While waiting for his mom to come out, he started looking for what he wanted to choose as his treat for the day. It appeared that he really didn't know what he wanted, but then he said he couldn't find it. His mom asked him what he wanted, and he said he wanted a "Sood Blocker" ... You all know what that is, right? ... Well, we didn't either.

His mom kept pointing out different options, but no—he wasn't interested in her suggestions. He was determined to get his Sood Blocker. He even knew where the label was, but it was no longer there. He tried explaining to us—his mom, his brother, and me—what a Sood Blocker was. He became so frustrated that he even began to cry because we didn't understand what he wanted.

I eventually figured out what he wanted, but I just wanted to have a little more fun with the situation, so I dragged it out a little longer. At the time, we had a popsicle that was black cherry ice on the outside with a cherry sauce center. The picture of it was a black popsicle with one corner bitten off, revealing the red inside. The name of that popsicle was "Dracula." The black represented Dracula's cape, and the red was the blood. That's the one Sean wanted that day. Another name for that popsicle, in his mind, was the "Blood Sucker," as he sometimes referred to it. But instead of saying "Blood Sucker," he kept saying "Sood Blocker." Now we knew. I had run out of the Dracula popsicle, so I had taken the picture down.

Realizing that his apparent pre-planned choice would not be an option that day, he started to accept his disappointment. As he began calming down from his frustration and tears, he slowly started wiping his face and began looking for another option. He ended up getting a Screwball. With tears still dripping down his face, Sean went on his merry way—another thrilling moment at the ice cream truck for Sean. For Sean, it was just another day, and he could hardly wait for tomorrow.

That memory alone is enough to last a lifetime, but I can't tell that story without sharing another memorable moment with Sean.

May 28, 1976

Peter Palagi
Palagi Ice Cream Co.
55 Bacon Street
Pawtucket, R. I.

Dear Peter:

It was with a great deal of regret that I learned of
your retirement today. The picture and news article
in this morning's Providence Journal really brought
back fond memories of my childhood.

My days go back beyond the 1930 Fords which have really
become an institution in the City of Pawtucket. I can
recall reaching up for my cone of ice cream (which I
believe went for 2 for five cents then) when it was
being brought around the neighborhood by horse and
wagon.

Your father really brought a great deal of joy to the
kids (and the adults) for many years and then you and
Phil took over. I can still hear the kids yelling,
"Here comes Peter Palagi"! - what a truly magnificent
sound! Clang, clang, clang went the bell! Then we would
all scamper home to see if dear old mom could scrounge
up a nickle on a hot summer night - and many the time
she had to disappoint us. But that was okay - we could
always settle for a couple of licks from the kid next
door.

Pleasant St., Tower St., Taft St., Rhodes St., Cleveland
St., and so many others that you traveled on - so many
miles - will never be the same without you.

You, Phil and those wonderful old trucks, which the kids
still run after today certainly became a real significant
part of my youth which we all refer to as, "The good old
days"!

Thanks so much for all the hours you put in, the thousands
of miles you traveled, the millions of times you rang the
bell and the ready smile you always had for all of us.

Peter Palagi              -2-              May 28, 1976

We all owe you and Phil a great deal and since all good
things have to come to an end - let me extend to you
Peter, and Phil, my profound gratitude for giving me
such fond memories to cherish and look back on.

My very best wishes to both of you for a well deserved
long, healthy and happy retirement. You have truly
earned it.

                              Sincerely,

                              *Frank Lyons*

                              FRANK J. LYONS
                              Corning Glass Works
                              1193 Broad Street
                              Central Falls, R.I.
                              02863

On another occasion, here comes the ice cream man approaching the house. Like clockwork, Sean comes out with the same excitement and enthusiasm he displayed the day before—actually, every day. As he's waiting for his mom, he begins looking around to see what he will choose that day. Now standing in front of the truck, Sean seemed to be quite a bit more excited on this day than his usual solid 10. He was a consistent 10 daily, but on this day, his excitement level was like a 10 on steroids—times ten!

When Sean's mom came out, he could hardly contain himself; he was so excited to be getting ice cream... again, just like every other day.

But this day was different. He started running circles around his mom, grabbing her skirt, and—as the saying goes— almost jumping out of his skin. Almost losing control in his excitement, he was still running around, clearly happy that I was there... well, maybe not necessarily that I was there, but that the ice cream truck was. I just happened to be the man responsible for the truck being there every day, and he really appreciated me for that.

Still caught up in his excitement and not really knowing what to do with himself, it seemed like he truly wanted to express his appreciation for me bringing ice cream every day. Not knowing exactly how to do it, he gave me the best compliment any ice cream man could ever get. Actually, I don't know if any other ice cream man has ever received such a compliment. He looked at me and said, "you cook good food!"

I don't think his mom, his brother Joseph, or I will ever forget that.

Like Sean's story, there are thousands upon thousands more in the memories of Rhode Islanders about the magic of the ice cream truck!

# 6

# THE ICE CREAM TRUCKS TODAY

Today, Palagis Ice Cream Company has 20 trucks. We are licensed in 25 out of 39 Rhode Island cities and towns, from Woonsocket at its northern border to North Kingstown and everywhere in between, also covering some towns in the East Bay—Barrington, Warren, Bristol, Portsmouth, and Middletown.

We receive many special requests for events such as family gatherings, school events, fundraisers, corporate events, employee appreciation, daycare centers, summer programs, and sports leagues, along with some unexpected requests that surprise us. In recent years, we have fulfilled over 1,600 special requests annually.

Daily, each truck serves between 200 and 400 people, averaging around 250 to 300 customers per day. At 250 people per truck across 20 trucks, that amounts to approximately 5,000 people visiting our trucks daily. But it's not just 5,000 people—it's 5,000 moments. Special moments. It's like magic when the truck shows up. *Five thousand magical moments.* I feel it is my responsibility, my privilege, my job, and my purpose to make sure that **MAGIC** happens each and every day.

*Model-A Ford at company headquarters
in the process of restoration.*

*Peter Palagi, Jr. serving customers.*

## PALAGIS ICE CREAM SHACK

In 2020, the year of the pandemic, we opened Palagis Ice Cream Shack at company headquarters—a place where you can enjoy an ice cream with family and friends while learning about the history of our company. There is a large patio area where we hold community events, including a weekly live music series, which we offer free to the community as part of our theme: *A Gift to the Community.*

*Palagis Ice Cream Shack on music series night.*

# 7

# I KNOW WHERE I AM...
# HOW DID I GET HERE?

## HOW DID I END UP AT PALAGIS ICE CREAM COMPANY? DESTINY, PERHAPS?

When meeting new people and the subject of what I do comes up, I tell them that I work at Palagis Ice Cream, and people's eyes light up. There is something about the word *ice cream* that just makes people feel good. When the word *ice cream* is in the same sentence as *Palagis*, there's a whole different and good feeling about it. When it comes to Palagis Ice Cream, most people have some fond memories.

They think it's the coolest thing. They come up with all kinds of comments, stories, and, yes, questions. Among the many questions that come up, the one I often get is: *How did I end up at Palagis Ice Cream?* People are curious—it's a common question.

Well, my brother Oscar worked there for a few summers after finishing high school. His girlfriend at the time was Lisa Palagi, and her father was Ronnie Palagi, who was Donald's cousin.

Ronnie worked in Cumberland, Rhode Island, selling ice cream for about 40 years. Everybody in town knew Ronnie Palagi, the ice cream man. Needless to say, Lisa was in the Palagi family. Oscar and Lisa went on to get married.

Learning from my brother's experience, I realized this was not just a job but an actual business that could be quite fruitful if you dedicated yourself to it and committed to the long hours required to make a business successful. The long hours didn't bother me.

On my brother's last season, I filled in for him for a few weeks at the end of that season, and then I came back the following year and took on a full-time route. So that's the story of how I got involved. It was as simple as that... or so I thought. *That's the short story.*

## HOW DID I END UP AT PALAGIS ICE CREAM COMPANY? THE LONG STORY.

As it turns out, there's a whole lot more to the story that I had not even thought about or realized. I had wanted to write this story for some time, picking up bits and pieces over the years while at the same time creating my own story in the history of this 100-plus-year-old company.

It's been 25 years for me as the owner of this beloved company. Not that 25 years was a magic number, but for some reason, I felt that after completing that milestone, I had earned my place in this history. It was time for me to tell the story... *Their story... My story... The whole story.*

I decided to put pen to paper with hopes of publishing it into a book. I had never done such a thing, but hey, there have been many other things I've done that I had never done before. There's always a first.

I believe the hardest thing about any project is just getting started, which reminds me of a quote: *"The journey of a thousand miles begins with a single step."* And I will add to that, *"That first single step is the most important and often the most difficult one."*

Another quote from Walt Disney comes to mind *"The best way to get started is to quit talking and start doing."*

So here I went—deciding to write my story.

In the process of researching certain information for this story, I started noticing some similarities between key dates in the history of Palagis Ice Cream Company and key dates in my own life. My life's trajectory seemed to align at some pivotal points in the life of Palagis Ice Cream Company, leading one to wonder if all this was just a coincidence... or maybe something deeper than that... like destiny, perhaps?

Peter Palagi Sr. named his youngest son Peter Palagi. My father's name was Alejandro Arteaga, and he named his youngest son Alejandro Arteaga—which was me.

Palagis Ice Cream Company was started in 1896 by Peter Palagi Sr. It was owned by three generations of the Palagi family for 102 years until 1998 when I took ownership of the company.

After 35 years in business, the company began the era of the now-famous Model A Ford ice cream trucks in 1931. These trucks were the face of the company for 50 years until 1981.

The birth year of these trucks was 1931, which was also the year my father was born—some 2,500 miles away in Colombia, South America. The year of my father's passing was 1981. He was 49 years old, and we were living in Cumberland, Rhode Island, at the time. He did not make it to his 50th birthday, but he was in his 50th year. My father's lifespan was the same as the lifespan of the Model A Fords—1931 to 1981.

These were the first dates that I noticed that matched up.

## MY JOURNEY TO PALAGIS ICE CREAM COMPANY

Peter Jr. and his brothers—Philip, Eduard, and Henri—who had owned the company since the late 1940s, purchased the property on Bacon Street in Pawtucket, Rhode Island, in July 1966 to build the ice cream company plant at that location. Ironically, some 2,500 miles away, I was born in July 1966—the same year and the same month the Bacon Street property was purchased, where the company still stands today.

Ten years later, in 1976, Peter Jr.'s son, Donald, bought the company and became the third-generation family member to run it. The summer of 1976 was Donald's first season managing the business. That same summer, in June 1976, I arrived from Colombia and settled in Cumberland, Rhode Island, with my family.

Donald ran the company until 1998, when I took ownership. Looking back now, it almost seems as if Peter Jr.'s son, Donald, took over the company in 1976—the same year I arrived in the U.S.—and held onto it until I was ready to take over. Company headquarters remained at the Bacon Street property, which had been purchased in 1966—the year of my birth. Not only was it purchased in the year of my birth, but it was bought in the exact same month: July 1966.

In the late 1960s and throughout the 1970s, there was a wave of immigrants coming from Colombia to Rhode Island. Almost everyone from Colombia during that time settled in Central Falls. The city of Central Falls is separated from the town of Cumberland by a river, with the bridge serving as the town line. When you cross the river from Central Falls, you enter Cumberland.

When we arrived in the U.S. in 1976, despite most Colombians settling in Central Falls, my father—who had already been here since 1972—rented an apartment on the other side

*Pawtucket Hall of Fame induction night
for Peter, Donald, and me.*

of the bridge, in the first house in Cumberland. My family's decision to settle in Cumberland instead of Central Falls was a key event in my journey to Palagis Ice Cream Company.

It kind of reminds me of the movie *Back to the Future*— as if, had we moved into an apartment in Central Falls instead, it would have altered the sequence of events, changing everything about my future. Who knows where I would have ended up? It's highly unlikely I would have found my way to Palagis Ice Cream Company, or even if the company itself would still be around today. Everything would have been different.

We settled in Cumberland, and my siblings and I were all enrolled in local schools. I attended St. Patrick's School with my sister Gloria, just up the street. My brother Oscar went to South Cumberland Middle School.

After middle school, Oscar continued on to Cumberland High School, where he met Lisa Palagi. Lisa's father was

Ronnie Palagi, Donald's cousin. Since Oscar was dating Lisa, he was somewhat connected to the family, even though they weren't married at the time. That connection eventually led him to work at Palagis Ice Cream Company—paving the way for me to end up there as well.

So, through my brother Oscar's connection to the Palagi family, I found my own path to the company. That's the long story of how I got there. Had we not settled in Cumberland, my brother would never have met Lisa Palagi. If he hadn't met Lisa, he wouldn't have worked at Palagis. If he hadn't worked there, I wouldn't have followed him. All these seemingly small moments had to align perfectly for me to eventually end up working at Palagis Ice Cream Company—and, ultimately, take ownership of it. The dots connected at different stages of my life, all leading me to where I am today.

## A HYPOTHETICAL

As it is difficult to predict anyone's destiny—unless, perhaps, you're in the royal family—let's pretend for a moment that I had been born into the Palagi family, some 2,500 miles away. The Palagi family, looking forward to the future with hopes of keeping the business thriving well beyond the next generation, placed all their faith in an addition to the family who was already on the way. With that in mind, they purchased the property on Bacon Street in Pawtucket, Rhode Island, in the same year and the same month that the new addition to the family would arrive—July 1966.

That addition to the family was a baby—me—born 2,500 miles away in the same year and the same month that the property was purchased, a property that would become the future headquarters of the family business. Nearly 60 years later, it remains the company headquarters.

After establishing the headquarters for the ice cream company on that site, ten years later, it was time for Peter and his brother Philip to retire. The addition to the family was just ten years old and obviously not yet ready to take on the responsibility of running the company. In the interim, Peter's son, Donald, took ownership of the company in 1976. In the middle of the summer of that same year, that ten-year-old boy arrived from a faraway land and settled in the town of Cumberland, where Donald lived. While Donald was running the company, the young boy was going through the normal stages of life—going to school, playing sports, socializing, and eventually graduating from high school.

A couple of years after high school, having attended college for one year, it was time to join the family business and begin the apprenticeship of running the company. Donald continued to run the business until 1998, when that young boy—now a responsible, reliable, and capable young man—was ready to take ownership and lead the company as a fourth-generation member.

It almost seems as if Donald, having taken over the company in 1976—the same summer that boy arrived from his native land—was merely taking care of the business until that boy was ready. That boy, who was born in the same year and the same month that the property for the company headquarters was purchased—as if the property had been acquired for him upon his birth, to carry the company into the future.

## COINCIDENCE OR DESTINY? HMMM...

I haven't even mentioned the fact that my father was born in 1931—2,500 miles away—the same year that the Model A Ford ice cream trucks were purchased, symbolizing a rebirth of sorts for the company and its future. One of those 1931

Model A Ford ice cream trucks remains at company head-quarters today. The lifespan of those trucks mirrored the lifespan of my father's life.

All of these facts, combined with the fact that we settled in Cumberland when nearly all other Colombians arriving at that time settled in Central Falls, kind of makes you wonder... Was I born with this predetermined destiny? I don't believe in that... but it really does make you wonder.

That, my friends, is the long story of how I ended up at Palagis Ice Cream Company.

Here in 2024, the coincidences continue. I began the resto-ration of that old 1931 Model A Ford truck that has remained at company headquarters. In a sense, I am bringing it back to life after it lay dormant for over 40 years. It has been sitting inside the Bacon Street ice cream warehouse since 1981—the year of my father's passing.

When this book is complete, and people begin to read it—reading stories about my father—in a sense, it will be as if my father is coming back to life after being dormant for over 40 years. His story continues. When people pass away, their sto-ries do not die with them; they live on—through their children and through the people who knew them.

After all, his story is my story. And vice versa. My story is his story.

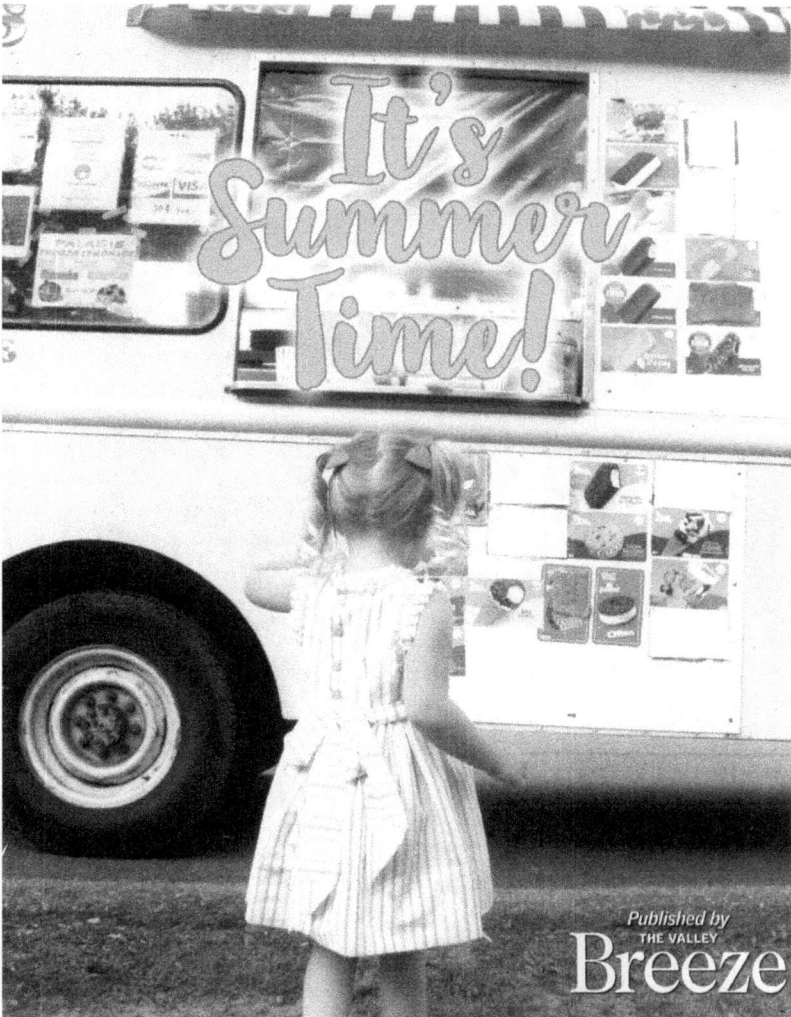

It's Summer Time!

Published by
THE VALLEY
Breeze

# John Hanlon

## Peter Palagi's trucks are considered 'institutions'

PAWTUCKET — This will be mainly about the Peter Palagi ice cream trucks, those wonderful Model A Fords that would be museum pieces if they were not still the keystone of the old-line business here of ~~80~~ years standing. *102 YEARS*

If you have not had a Peter Palagi truck bell its way along your street of a summer night, hailing children of all ages with its brass bell clanging, then you must have lived a long way off. There are six of them (plus seven "new" trucks), the most ancient of which is a 1930, the "youngest" a 1934. It staggers the sweet tooth to contemplate how many sundaes, cones, fudgicles, cannonballs and boxes of slush this represents to Rhode Island tummies. The trucks are square and blocky, and painted a splended golden hue, with blue trim and fancy lettering in red, all so varnished over that they gleam. Don Palagi, the 40-year-old, third-generation owner as of this summer, was saying at the plant yesterday why they have kept them in mint condition and on the road these many years. "Well, they are known, first of all." Don said, "and when kids hear the bell they come running.

*Don Palagi*

They are conversation pieces. People send us cards and fan mail, and tell stories about them. And let's face it, a new truck equipped costs $12,500. We can maintain the old ones for about $200 each a year."

It helps mightily that this maintenance is a labor of love and skill done mostly by Don's father, Peter Jr., with some help from Uncle Phil Palagi. These two had taken over from the senior Peter, who began the business in 1896 out of his house where the Apex store now stands to augment his vegetable trade. He began with a pushcart, went to the trucks in 1930. He bought only the chassis from Ford and had the bodies custom built by a blacksmith named Baker in Seekonk.

Anyway, Don arranged that I go out with Dan McDermott in old No.1, the original Palagi truck. Dan is a junior at URI and works the truck under lease; except for some "independents," this is standard. When he finished loading, I climbed over the "counter" that filled the right-hand door for my first Model A ride in decades.

As usual with these critters, it flooded and wouldn't start. But after the mandatory rest, it caught and we putt-putted away. You really know you are motoring in a Model A, far above those ridiculously sleek vehicles below. You sway a lot, but, then, you don't go very fast. And when Dan got to his business area, he crawled his machine along about four or five miles an hour—in high gear! Try that on your Chevy or Ford.

It was a little early to catch the out-of-school trade, but there were some toddlers who stepped right up on the running board. (Dad, please explain "running board," will you?). And as Don had said, people want to talk. A woman told of a youngster who had gone to Maine on a trip with her father and asked, "Do you suppose Peter Palagi will be in Maine?" The child suffered a broken shoulder there and, back here in the hospital, was pleased to hear the familiar bell again.

Back at the plant, Don showed a child's drawing of their truck, and he had a letter from a man who remembered the senior Palagi's horsedrawn wagon, and spoke of the trucks as "an institution." Things like that.

Six Palagi relatives are among the current leassees or independents, and Don's 14-year-old son, Chris, helps make ice cream part-time. At one point, after he finished at URI in 1961, Don left for other fields. Last year, when his father offered to sell, Don said he thought "long and deep." But he came back, "because it was there in me." For a Palagi, it really couldn't have been otherwise.

BIOGRAPH

*April 16* **Peter Palagi Jr.** *1990*

*Ice cream vendor*

**Born/Resides:** Lifelong of Pawtucket, born 9/22/10, youngest boy of 14 children of Pietro and Severina (Peter and Sarah) Palagi of Borgo Morzano, Luca, Italy. All born in fieldstone house where Apex is now.

Peter Palagi Jr.

**Family business:** "We worked together, the whole family, girls and boys" for Palagi's Ice Cream, est. 1896.

**Education:** Division St. School to grade 4, Grove St. School to grade 8, "and then I got out."

**Starting out:** "I was peddling ice cream at 9 years old with the horse and wagon" built by D.F. Baker, Seekonk, with roll-down curtains and slit for reins. "We had 10 horses. My old pet was 'Tom.' We had a few runaways in those days. The horse showed me the route." 4-9 p.m. after school, all day summers, 7 days/wk.

**Vehicles:** Switched to 4-cylinder Model A's modeled after the wagons in 1929 (retain one, with 800,000 mi.). Now have 11 GMC and Ford ice cream trucks.

**Innovation:** "We were the first in R.I. to make popsicles," two for a nickel and twice as big 40 years ago as now.

**Old days:** "Kids had nowheres to go then. They were always around" and behaved "wonderful." Robbed once, of $12, "at the watering trough on Central Avenue. He said he had a gun ... My father always told me to give them the money." He was 11.

**Set your watch:** "We had a regular route and we tried to be on time, same time every day. We didn't have to ring the bell. They were standing on the corner waiting. If the truck didn't come down, the phone would ring off the hook."

**Favorite flavor:** "Strawberry years ago, when I was younger, now chocolate. I really love chocolate." Sells five flavors, 18 novelties.

**Ice cream mix:** Was "from scratch" with cream, eggs, sugar, stabilizer, milk, "a little water too and your flavors." But now they use Hood's.

**Changes:** People in '30s brought bowls for ice cream — 25 cents got 3 scoops extra. Still sell hand-scooped cones.

**Prices:** In 1940, large banana split "with 3 scoops of ice cream, whipped cream, nuts, everything" was 10 cents, double cones a nickel. Double cones now $1.25.

**Season starts:** Officially, Easter, but "We've had some good St. Patrick's Days."

**Hobby:** "This is my hobby, the business. How can you have a hobby when you work 7 days a week?"

**Routes:** Pawtucket, Central Falls, Barrington, Mansfield, Warwick, Attleboro.

**Not the retiring type:** "I retired in '75. But I never retired. I'm in every day." In summer, works 3 a.m.-2 p.m. "unless a truck breaks down."

**Family:** Wife Mary (D'Ambra); son Don, now runs Palagi's; son Peter III ("He never liked the ice cream business"), USAF Col. and pharmacist in Texas.

**By Douglas Hadden**
*The Evening Times staff*

## n: A cool 100 summers

Submitted photo

CHILDHOOD MEMORIES — Peter Palagi Jr. dishes out treats in the waning days of summer in 1965. The company was still located near the Main Street Bridge in Pawtucket, and would relocate in 1968 to make way for the Apex parking lot.

—Journal-Bulletin Photo by CANDACE FREELAND

COOLING OFF: Oscar Arteaga of Cumberland sells ice cream and frozen lemonade from a converted Model T Ford outside Bishop Francis P. Keough School in Pawtucket after summer school classes let out.

*My brother Oscar driving one of
the Model-A Ford trucks*

*Peter Palagi and Rod*

*Peter Palagi Senior*

# SEARCHING FOR PETER PALAGI

## "AN AMERICAN LEGEND"

### THE SEARCH FOR PURPOSE

# PARKER'S STORY

## A CHILDREN'S TALE

P arker is an ice cream lover and a Palagis Ice Cream customer.

Patrick and Paul are teachers in their hometown of Bangor, Maine. They have known each other since kindergarten, both born in the same year, 1935. They have been lifelong friends, going through every stage of life together. The only time they spent apart was when they went their separate ways for college.

Paul loved the ocean, while Patrick loved the mountains. Their passions were developed as children, mainly from their family vacations, and played a major role in deciding where they would attend college.

Paul and his family often visited Rhode Island on their summer vacations, spending time at the famous beaches of Narragansett and Newport. They also visited the capital city of Providence and its neighboring historic city, Pawtucket. Pawtucket is most famous for being the birthplace of the Industrial Revolution and later became well known for McCoy Stadium. Paul was a baseball fan, as was Patrick, and visiting McCoy Stadium as a child during Rhode Island vacations became a tradition for Paul.

Patrick's passion for the mountains was also established in childhood while vacationing in New Hampshire's White

Mountain region. He loved skiing, though most of his visits were in the summer. He also enjoyed hiking, exploring rivers that flowed down from the mountains, and finding crystal-clear pools surrounded by beautiful rocks for jumping, diving, and swimming.

Paul was drawn to the ocean and everything associated with it, so he thought, what better place to go to college than "The Ocean State"? He chose Rhode Island College, where he could enjoy the ocean and catch a few baseball games while studying. Patrick, wanting to be near the mountains, he chose Keene State College in New Hampshire. They both graduated in 1957.

After college, they returned home and became teachers at the same local high school—Paul as a history teacher and Patrick as a physical education teacher.

Paul loved history and historic places, making his job as a history teacher a natural fit. He loved his work. Patrick, on the other hand, seemed to enjoy his job but was not very vocal about it. Despite their different teaching subjects, they shared many similarities: growing up in the same town, their love for baseball, and a shared fondness for ice cream.

About 15 years after college, having established their careers, they decided to visit Rhode Island on their summer break. It was the Fourth of July weekend in 1972. They spent the morning and part of the afternoon at the beach, then attended a baseball game at McCoy Stadium in Pawtucket, where a fireworks display was planned after the game in celebration of Independence Day.

With so many people attending, parking was scarce. They eventually found a spot on a side street behind the stadium and made a mental note of its name: Bacon Street.

After the game and fireworks, they headed back to their car. As they walked down Bacon Street, they saw a strange-looking truck approaching. It was an old, antique truck with a bell ringing noise. The driver greeted them warmly, but they still weren't sure what to make of it—until they noticed the words "ice cream" on the side. It was an ice cream truck!

Coming from Maine, they had heard of ice cream trucks but had never seen one in person. They excitedly lined up and picked out their treats. As they enjoyed their ice cream, they overheard others talking about the man inside the truck, referring to him as "Peter." The truck had "Peter Palagi Ice Cream" written on it. Moments later, another truck with the same name passed by—then another.

It turned out that the Peter Palagi Ice Cream Company had its headquarters right there on Bacon Street, behind the stadium. Paul, amused by the coincidence, remarked, "I like bacon, and I like ice cream. Here we have ice cream on Bacon Street!"

People around the truck mentioned that Peter Palagi had been in the ice cream business since the early 1900s, originally selling ice cream from horse-drawn wagons. Some even claimed he was the first ice cream man. It was the perfect ending to an already extraordinary day.

Patrick and Paul continued teaching at the same school until they retired in 1996. A year later, Paul visited Rhode Island. In the fall of the following year, a couple of years after retiring, they went on a drive with no particular destination, as they had done many times before, chatting about life and current events.

During the drive, Paul said, "Now that I'm retired, I can finally do what I've always wanted to do."

Patrick, puzzled but curious, asked, "Yeah? What's that, Paul?"

Paul responded, "I'd like to get in a van, drive around the country, visit all the places I've always read about, and revisit places I've been to before. We can go to New Hampshire to see your mountains, visit historic Massachusetts and Boston—including Fenway Park—spend a few days in Rhode Island at the beaches, and maybe even stop by that baseball stadium and the ice cream company if they're still around. Then we can head to New York City, Washington, D.C., and see where the road takes us."

It all sounded exciting to Patrick, but he hesitated. "Whoa, whoa, whoa—slow down. You keep saying 'we,' but you haven't even asked if I want to go."

Paul smiled. "Well, we've always done everything together, and I wouldn't want to go without you."

Patrick admitted, "It sounds like fun, but I'd need to think about it and plan. Being away from home for so long would be expensive, and honestly, I'm not sure I can afford it."

Patrick knew that Paul had always been disciplined—with his work and his money. He admired Paul for his dedication, especially how passionate he was about teaching. Patrick reflected on this and said, "You always talked about how much you loved your job and how it gave you a sense of purpose. I liked my job, but I never thought about it the way you do. For me, it was just a way to make a living—I never considered it a passion or something that could make a real difference in my students' lives."

Paul could not believe what he was hearing. He said, "Are you serious? Not only did you teach physical education, emphasizing the importance of exercising, staying in shape, and maintaining strength and health, but you also coached the school's baseball team for almost 40 years. You have no idea how much of a difference you have made in your students' lives, especially those you coached."

Paul continued, "I was there at many of your games when you were coaching. Let me remind you of all the championships you won—experiences of a lifetime for those kids. But more importantly, I remember the days when your teams lost 'The Big Game.' When the kids were heartbroken and down, your words and speeches lifted them up, giving them hope to fight another day. You taught them that there is much more to learn from one tough loss than from 20 victories."

Listening to all this, Patrick began to feel pretty good about his life's work and the impact he had on his students and players. Reflecting, he thought to himself, *Yeah, I did have passion for my work, and yes, I did fulfill my purpose by contributing to and changing the lives of many students and players.*

Now that they had moved beyond discussing their work and contributions to their communities, Patrick and Paul shifted the conversation to finances. Patrick admitted that, while he wasn't bad with money, he wasn't as good as Paul, especially when it came to saving for the future and retirement.

"I started thinking about finances early on when I began working," Paul told Patrick. "My parents always reminded me of the importance of saving early."

Paul went into teacher mode, wanting to reiterate some of the financial lessons his parents had taught him. "They told me that, over time, money grows through the accumulation of interest and the power of compound interest."

"They also taught me that different people have different ideas about money. Some people accumulate it to buy luxurious, expensive things because that makes them feel good. But they emphasized that the most valuable thing money can buy is peace of mind. The idea that when an emergency arises— not *if* but *when* because it will—you can afford to get through it without financial stress."

Paul continued, "I know I sound like I'm preaching, but I'm just sharing the valuable lessons I was taught. Another important lesson my parents stressed was putting yourself in a position to help someone in need. It's incredibly satisfying to be able to help when the need arises. That doesn't necessarily mean handing out money—though at times that may be the best option—but having financial stability allows you to buy *time*. When you're not struggling to make ends meet, you have the time to help others."

"And the third lesson," Paul added, "was that financial security gives you the ability to do what you truly want. Right now, I want to take this trip, driving around the country, and I want my good friend along for the ride."

"Don't worry about the finances," Paul reassured Patrick. "This is exactly what I've saved for my whole life—to be able to enjoy retirement without financial worries."

Patrick listened intently, absorbing Paul's wisdom. At the same time, he felt a little regretful that he hadn't received the same advice in his younger years. He wished he were in the same financial position as Paul.

Paul then shared a wise saying: "You can't go back and change the beginning, but you can start where you are and change the ending." In other words, the past is the past, but the future is still within one's control.

He continued, "You can always improve your story and cement your legacy. You may feel like you're closer to the end, but I remind you that when one dies, their story doesn't end. It continues through their children, grandchildren, and the people who love them."

Paul shared another saying: "You live, you learn, you pass it on." He was as passionate about teaching as he was about learning. "Throughout life, we learn valuable lessons that help us along the way. We shouldn't be selfish with those lessons but instead pass them on to the next generation."

After their ride, Patrick accepted Paul's invitation to go on the ultimate road trip to explore their beloved country. They decided that early April 1999, after winter had passed, would be the perfect time.

A couple of years earlier, Paul had visited Rhode Island. While driving through the East Side of Providence, he stopped at Lippitt Park. That day, an ice cream truck arrived, and being an ice cream lover, Paul stepped up to get a treat. There, he met Parker, Patti, and their parents. Parker and Patti were best friends who met at the park a few years prior and often met there after school. Parker was usually with his grandpa, while Patti was accompanied by her mom.

The ice cream truck was like a magnet, drawing people together. Just seeing it lifted everyone's spirits. The name on the truck was *Palagis Ice Cream.* That name triggered a memory for Paul from 25 years earlier when he visited Rhode Island with Patrick.

Paul introduced himself: "Hello, my name is Paul. Love the ice cream truck! What are your names?"

Patti responded for the group, "I'm Patti, and this is my friend Parker," pointing to him. "And that is my mom and Parker's grandpa."

"Nice to meet you all," Paul said. "I'm visiting from Maine. I went to college in Rhode Island and have been back a few times. I *love* the ice cream truck. That name—Palagis Ice Cream—reminds me of a visit some 25 years ago when my best friend and I went to a baseball game at McCoy Stadium. Do you know about McCoy Stadium?"

Parker's grandpa replied, "Yes, we know it's in Pawtucket, but we've never been. We're not big on baseball."

Paul chuckled. "Well, it's a nice place. You should go sometime. But it's not about the stadium—it's the name on that truck. That name brought back memories. It was Independence Day, the 4th of July, and the stadium was sold out. That night, there was a fireworks display after the game in celebration of the holiday. After the fireworks, we went to find our car on a side street where we had left it. On that street, we saw an old antique ice cream truck with the name "Peter Palagi Ice Cream" on it. We weren't sure if it was the same company, but it was the name "Palagi" that stood out and brought back memories. That was a great night.

Paul continued telling his story. "When we were talking with some folks who were also getting ice cream, a second truck identical to the one we were at drove by with the same name, 'Peter Palagi Ice Cream'... and then a third. It turned out that the Peter Palagi Ice Cream Company headquarters was on that street—Bacon Street. I even remember the name of the street. My friend and I had commented on it so that we would remember how to find our car after the game. I said, 'I like bacon, and I like ice cream, and here we have ice cream on Bacon Street!' We never forgot the name of that street."

As the ice cream truck pulled away, we continued our conversation with the other people getting ice cream. They told us that Peter Palagi had been the ice cream man for a long, long time. They actually knew that the man serving them was Peter himself. They would refer to him as Peter and even said they thought he was the first ice cream man.

Paul's conversation was mostly with Patti's mom and Parker's grandpa, but Patti and Parker were listening to every word with fascination.

"That's a great story," Patti's mom said. "Parker and Patti seemed to really enjoy it. They love the ice cream truck."

Patti's mom asked, "Isn't that right, kids?"

Patti and Parker both nodded and responded, "Yes, we love it!"

Parker added, "It's the same truck that goes to both our schools."

Patti chimed in, "That's one of the main reasons we come to this playground. The ice cream truck comes here all the time too."

Paul ended up hanging around, getting to know the kids, playing Frisbee, and having fun with them at the playground until it was time to go.

Paul's parting words were, "I'm thinking of coming back this way sometime next year with my friend. It would be great to see you guys again and check in on the progress of the kids."

Addressing the parents, Paul asked, "If you don't mind sharing your number, I'll let you know when I'll be back."

Patti's mom responded, "Sure, that's not a problem." They exchanged numbers, said goodbye, and went their separate ways.

Parker and Patti really enjoyed meeting Paul. They were mesmerized by his story about his run-in with the ice cream truck almost a quarter of a century ago, especially his encounter with not just an ice cream man, but possibly America's first ice cream man.

Peter Palagi—a name that would stick in their minds. They would always be reminded of that name every time they got ice cream from the truck. It was always Palagis Ice Cream truck—the one they always seemed to run into, or at least one of the Palagis Ice Cream trucks, as there seemed to be more than one, as they saw others in different colors.

A couple of years later, after Paul had visited Rhode Island and met Parker, Patti, and their parents in Providence, Paul and Patrick were ready to go on the adventurous road trip of a lifetime.

They first set out towards New Hampshire's White Mountain region. Paul knew how much Patrick loved the mountains. They spent some time in the famous village of North Conway, in the town of Conway. After that, they visited the

Mount Washington Cog Railway—the world's first moun-
tain-climbing cog railway. After stopping at the Cog Railway,
they crossed the Kancamagus Highway and visited the town
of Lincoln, New Hampshire, before heading south toward
Massachusetts. All these places had been part of Patrick's
playground, especially during his college days when he lived
there.

During their three-day stay in Massachusetts, they visited
the John F. Kennedy Library as well as a couple of museums—
the Museum of Fine Arts and the Museum of Science—since
Paul was a big fan of museums. All these museum stops and
the historic sites in Boston were really Paul's cup of tea. They
had also planned their trip to coincide with Opening Day for
the Boston Red Sox at Fenway Park. It was the first time they
had been able to attend Opening Day, something they had
always wanted to do—especially Patrick. After their visit to
New Hampshire, which pleased Patrick, and all the stops in
Boston, which pleased Paul, they both got a real treat—Boston Red Sox Opening Day at Fenway Park! They were thrilled
to be there, having the time of their lives.

Then it was time to visit Rhode Island, which Paul was
really looking forward to. For him, it was like going home since
he had lived there during his college days. Paul always thought
of Rhode Island as "the smallest state with the biggest heart."
He always felt the warmth and kindness of the people while
in Rhode Island.

It was a beautiful Friday in early April in the city of Providence—the kind of day that breaks record-high temperatures
for the season. It marked the beginning of a beautiful weekend, with a carbon-copy forecast for Saturday and Sunday.
It was one of the first truly nice days of spring, arriving early
in April. This rare early spring weather brought excitement
and a burst of energy, waiting to be used up and enjoyed.

Parents took advantage of the weather, bringing their children to their favorite playgrounds after school. Lippitt Park, on the East Side of Providence, was the perfect combination of playground and open space, allowing kids to run around and burn off energy.

Lippitt Park, located on Blackstone Boulevard, was buzzing with activity. There were lots of children playing on the playground and running around the spacious grassy area. This park was always busy after school, as it was surrounded by several schools in the area. Some children played alone under the watchful eyes of their parents, while others played in small groups. On this day, Parker and Patti were enjoying the beautiful weather and each other's company. Just by watching them play and run around, you could tell they had known each other for some time, as they were clearly comfortable together.

Parker was an African American 10-year-old and a 5th grader at Martin Luther King Jr. Elementary School in Providence. He lived with his family not far from where he went to school. He was a good student who kept up with all his homework assignments and made sure to study for tests. He was also a curious kid with a vivid imagination, often telling stories about dreams he had or books he had read. He loved to read.

He lived with his parents, his sister—a freshman at nearby Hope High School—and his grandfather. Their house was right around the corner from his school. Parker spent a lot of time with his grandfather since his parents worked long hours, often juggling two jobs to make ends meet.

Grandpa always encouraged Parker to do well in school, frequently asking how he was doing and reminding him to maintain his good grades. He told Parker that steady, consistent discipline would open up a world of opportunities for him.

"With this discipline, you can be whatever you want to be," he would say. "Reading and education are the keys to opening doors. Dream the dream, then wake up and make it happen. Believe that you can, and that's more than half the battle."

Grandpa also emphasized gratitude. "Don't worry about what you don't have—be grateful for what you do have, every little thing. People take too much for granted. Always appreciate when someone does something for you, and make sure to say 'thank you'—the two most powerful words in the English language. And don't just say it—mean it. If you ever get a chance to pay it forward, jump on it."

Grandpa was also an avid reader. Even though he did not receive any education beyond high school, he always felt he was an educated, curious, well-read man with good manners and empathy for people. He also possessed the ability to adapt to different situations, which, in his mind, formed the foundation of a good education. The rest of his education came from reading lots of books and life experiences. He once shared a quote from Bruce Lee with Parker that he really liked: "Instead of buying your children the things that you never had, you should teach them all the things that you were never taught. Material things wear out, but knowledge stays."

Parker's family had recently bought a house with the help of his grandfather. This was the first time his family had been able to save enough money for a down payment and qualify for a mortgage. His grandfather felt proud and grateful that he was able to help put the family in a better financial position. He knew that buying a home and beginning to build equity was a great step toward a better financial future.

Grandpa was also excited about having a garage where he could keep his tools and turn it into a workshop. He had worked in the construction industry building houses. He was a self-taught carpenter and enjoyed taking on projects, building things out of wood. Parker spent a lot of time watching Grandpa work and learning as much as he could from him. He was always teaching Parker his craft, but more importantly, he was teaching him the life lessons he had learned along the way.

Parker was a curious kid and always wanted to know what Grandpa was working on. One day, he asked, "Grandpa, what are you making?"

Grandpa responded, "I'm making some bookcases."

Parker asked, "Who are they for?"

"Not sure," Grandpa replied. "Eventually, someone will buy them. I have a friend who owns a furniture store, and he knows that I am a carpenter and can build anything he needs to sell in his store. He also knows that I do good work and take great pride in everything I do. So, he tells me what he needs and puts in an order with me. I'm not sure who will eventually buy them, but when I'm done, the bookcases will have a purpose. Everything has a purpose. That includes all things and all people—everyone and everything has a purpose."

Being the curious young man that he was, Parker asked, "Do kids have a purpose?"

Grandpa answered, "Of course they do. Like I said, everyone has a purpose. Some people don't think about it and don't even know what their purpose is, but everyone fits in somewhere and makes a difference. As a child, your first purpose is to do well in school and learn as much as you can about the world and how to get along with people while practicing good manners. Good manners are key to getting along with others. The more you learn, the better you get at making intelligent choices and becoming mentally independent and responsible. You also become aware of your ability to contribute and make a difference for the better—to make a positive impact in someone's life or for a cause. Eventually, even as a child, you may find something that you really care about and can make it your purpose or mission. A child should learn the lesson of leaving a place better than they found it. Once that lesson sinks in, you will find plenty of purpose to fulfill."

Parker listened closely. He then asked, "What about you, Grandpa? What is your purpose?"

"Well, son, my main purpose has always been to take care of my family—to always make sure I had a job so my family had a place to live, food on the table, and everything else we needed. That includes making sure we were able to buy a house. I also tried to teach my children everything I have learned along the way so they could avoid some of the mistakes I made and have a better future," Grandpa said. "I'm not sure how much longer I'll be around, but my story doesn't end when I die—my story continues through all of you."

Parker's best friend, Patti, was also a fifth grader but went to a different school. She lived with her family in the town of Barrington, Rhode Island. She also had an older brother who attended Barrington High School. Her mother was a professor at Brown University, where she had graduated from. Brown University was next to Moses Brown School, where Patti went, making it convenient for her mother to take her to school and pick her up. Moses Brown was one of the more prestigious schools in the state.

Patti's mom often tried to teach her lessons she had learned from experience, just as Parker's grandpa did with him. She taught her to see the world as a place with unlimited possibilities and emphasized the importance of connecting with others to build and nurture relationships.

Her father was a lawyer. Her mom was usually the one who picked her up from school and took her to the playground, where she had a chance to meet Parker's grandfather. They often chatted while the kids played.

The kids really enjoyed playing together at the playground, not only for fun but also because they looked forward to a visit from the ice cream truck. Patti and Parker were ice cream lovers and were convinced that ice cream always tasted better when bought from the ice cream truck—without a doubt!

The name on the truck was Palagis Ice Cream. It was the same truck that stopped by both of their schools. For the past few years, Parker and Patti had met at the playground, becoming best friends. They spent time at each other's houses and attended each other's birthday parties.

On this lovely early spring day, Parker and Patti visited their favorite playground once again. The start of spring also marked the beginning of the end of another school year. They ran around and played energetically, fueled by the extraordinary weather. Then, just as expected, the ice cream truck appeared—Palagis Ice Cream. They knew it well, and they even knew the driver. They didn't know his name, but his face was familiar—their favorite ice cream man. A true sign that spring had arrived!

Parker and Patti stepped up to the truck and each chose a treat. They asked the ice cream man if he would be back tomorrow, which was Saturday. He told them he would be there around noon and again later in the afternoon. Excited, Parker and Patti asked their parents if they could come back the next day. Wanting to see their kids happy, both parents agreed. The kids were thrilled. After enjoying their ice cream, they said their goodbyes and headed home.

Meanwhile, Paul and Patrick were on the highway, making their way into Rhode Island after visiting New Hampshire and some key locations in Boston they had always wanted to see.

As Paul always thought of Rhode Island as "the smallest state with the biggest heart," he imagined that one day, when passing the "Welcome to Rhode Island" sign, he would see a big, huge heart with the words "WELCOME TO RHODE ISLAND." Then that would really make it the smallest state with the biggest heart.

Upon arriving in Rhode Island, they visited Downtown Providence, exploring interesting parts of the city, including the ice skating rink, which was closing for the season. They also stopped by Brown University and had dinner on famous Thayer Street. While dining, they struck up a conversation with people at the next table, who suggested they visit the "WaterFire" event happening the next day. They also recommended Federal Hill on Atwells Avenue, known as "Providence's Little Italy." After dinner, Paul and Patrick checked into a hotel for the night, planning to visit Lippitt Park the next morning before heading to WaterFire in the evening.

After dinner, they checked into a hotel and stayed the night. Paul also remembered going to Blackstone Boulevard Park on the East Side and meeting some nice folks there as they gathered around the ice cream truck. He vividly remembered Parker and Patti. He also recalled that they had exchanged contact information so they could meet up when he came back. He had brought the contact information with him but had not called them yet. He figured he would call them at some point while he was here. Paul knew he wasn't far from the park, so he planned on stopping by the next day after spending the night in a hotel. Part of the plan for the following day, after visiting the park, was to do a little more sightseeing in the afternoon and then go to the famous "WaterFire," which had been mentioned in conversation with the folks they met at the restaurant.

Saturday arrived, bringing a bright, sunny sky without a cloud in sight. It was even warmer than the day before—spring had definitely arrived! Parker and Patti were fortunate that their parents were always willing to drive them around so they could be outside and socialize with other children. They had played hard the day before and had woken up tired, but that morning sun made anyone want to get up and go. So, they showed up at Lippitt Park around 10:00 AM. As soon as they met up, they immediately began running around and playing in the playground. Around noon, sure enough, the ice cream truck began making its way down the street, right on schedule. There was excitement in the air, as always, when the ice cream truck arrived. The truck started drawing people toward it, as if it were a magnet. You could literally see the joy on the faces of people walking toward it.

People gathered in front of the serving window, considering their options for a treat. Parker's favorite was a Two-Ball Screwball, which came in a cone-shaped, see-through plastic cup with sherbet ice cream and two gumballs at the bottom—an upgrade from the original Screwball, which had only one gumball. Patti chose a Chips Galore ice cream sandwich—vanilla ice cream between two chocolate chip cookies, with chocolate chips around the edges—a favorite for many. Patti's mom also got a treat as a little pick-me-up snack; she chose a Strawberry Shortcake, a popular choice among women. Parker's grandpa decided to indulge as well. His thought was, "Why not? It's here, I'm here, it's affordable, and I might as well treat myself." He chose a plain, old reliable ice cream sandwich.

As they finished making their selections and started to walk away, they noticed a familiar face—it was that nice man they had met a couple of years prior at the same spot. It was Paul, the teacher from Maine who had told them about his time attending school in Rhode Island. Everyone was delighted to see each other again. This time, Paul wasn't alone; he was with his friend Patrick, whom he introduced to everyone. They also got an ice cream treat and started chatting about what had been happening in their lives. They talked for a while and, before parting ways, made sure they still had each other's contact information for a future visit. It was time to go.

It was a warm, sunny day, and Parker was pretty worn out from all the running around. He asked his grandpa if he could rest a little before leaving. His grandpa allowed him just a few minutes, so Parker went behind a rock to find some shade and escape the hot sun for a bit of rest before heading home. Meanwhile, Grandpa was still chatting away with Paul and Patrick, and Patti and her mom were also still there.

Suddenly, Parker heard a voice.

"Hi there... I need a little help here."

Parker looked around but didn't see anyone. The voice called out again.

"Hey, down here!"

Parker looked down but still saw no one—just a trash barrel with some trash inside and some litter around it.

The voice spoke again.

"Here, under the trash barrel."

"I can't see you. There's no one there," Parker said.

"I need a hand," said the voice. "Yes, you're looking right at me—I'm the Hoodsie cup. Yes, the ice cream cup."

"What? You're not supposed to talk," Parker said in disbelief.

"Yes, I know. I'll explain. Can you please just help me get out from underneath this trash can?"

"This is really weird," Parker said. "I'll help you, and maybe you can make sense of this for me. Maybe I'm just dreaming. Let me see if I can help you."

Parker raised the trash can and pulled the Hoodsie cup out.

"Whew," said Hoodsie. "Thank you, young man. What is your name?"

"My name is Parker. What's going on here? Am I going crazy? I love ice cream, but I never thought it would talk to me and ask for a favor. How is that even possible?"

"Well, sometimes all it takes is just a wish or a thought about an object, and it finds a way to communicate," Hoodsie replied.

"Yeah, but I love ice cream, and you're not even ice cream—you're just the cup. The ice cream has been eaten, and you're just the cup that's been thrown away."

"Well, my friend, I'm not just the cup—I am 'THE CUP.' I have been granted immunity in my clan."

"What do you mean? Your clan? What is your clan?"

Hoodsie responded, "You know—my group, my family, my people... I love ice cream too."

Parker was puzzled. "You love ice cream too?"

"Of course I do. Ice cream is my family, and I love my family."

"You have a family?"

"Yes, of course. My family is my fellow ice cream novelties. We have ideas, plans, goals, and purpose."

"Purpose?" Parker interrupted.

"Yes—purpose, just like people have purpose. Everyone has a reason for being here. When they find out what that reason is, that's their purpose. Some people find out sooner than others, and some never find out or even care to. The people who do discover their purpose wake up each day with energy and excitement, eager to fulfill it."

"Well, if you say so," Parker said. "So now what? Anything else I can help you with?"

"I thought you'd never ask! Thanks for offering. I need your help."

"Well, I already helped you get out from under the trash can. What else do you need?"

"I need a ride."

"A ride? Are you kidding me? Is this a joke or something?"

"No, I'm very serious," Hoodsie replied.

"I'm not sure if I can help you or not. I'm still quite confused," Parker admitted.

"I know—it's a lot of information, and it doesn't really make sense."

"No, it doesn't," Parker said. "You mentioned that you had immunity and that you were 'THE CUP,' like you're special or something. Sorry, no offense, but I just don't get it."

Hoodsie responded, trying to make Parker understand. "That's okay, no offense taken. I know it's quite confusing. Unless you're in the clan, you wouldn't understand. Well, let me try to clarify it a little bit. Ice cream novelties are assembled and put in a freezer where they become frozen stiffs. Then they're packaged and placed into a box with some of their friends in groups of 12 or 24. Once that's done, they're ready to be served. So, from the time they are created to the time they are shipped to a place where they will be chosen (bought) and then eaten, that is the lifespan of that novelty item. At that point, they have fulfilled their purpose—to make people happy in their short life."

Parker interrupted. "Okay, I get all that... I guess. But what does all that have to do with you having immunity?"

"Well, I was getting to that, but you cut me off," Hoodsie replied before continuing. "When I say that I have been granted immunity, that means I have protection from that being the end of my life. My life continues, and I have a higher purpose. My higher purpose is to make sure that we, my clan, find the best representation to help us achieve our purpose. And yes, I am not just a cup. I am 'THE CUP,' one of the chosen few to ensure that we're all able to fulfill our purpose in the best way possible. The chosen ones are on the 'EXECUTIVE BOARD' of The Clan."

"Executive board?" Parker asked. "That sounds like a business. You guys are a family… sort of, I guess."

Hoodsie responded again. "You have to have some patience. I'm trying to tell you, but you keep cutting in."

"Sorry, it's just a lot of information."

"Where was I? Oh, right, the executive board. Yes, executive boards are for businesses, but actually, any group or organization can have an executive board to oversee strategic planning and decision-making."

Parker cut in again. "So I guess you're on that board?"

"I'm getting there," Hoodsie said, a bit annoyed.

Hoodsie continued. "The board consists of a group well-representative of the family. Even though we're all one big family and we're all ice cream novelties, each one of us has our own uniqueness, our own way of thinking, and thoughts about the world. The executive members are: The Strawberry Shortcake, representing the women; The Chocolate Éclair, representing the men; The Fudge Bar, who, even though they are complainers and picky, often have a good point; The Nutty Buddy, who's a little crazy but personable—everybody's friend. Everyone seems to have a buddy who is a bit nutty.

Then there is The Italian Ice. He's cool, and he brings high-intensity emotion to our meetings and our group. There's me, the Hoodsie Cup, representing the children of the clan—basically all the other Hoodsie Cups. Those are the children.

We also needed a few characters, so we have SpongeBob, Spider-Man, and Dora the Explorer. Then there is our leader, The Choco Taco…

Oops, I almost forgot! How could anyone forget Mr. Ice Cream Sandwich? He's the most reliable, responsible, and humble of the bunch. Whenever you're in doubt, that's who you look for. You can't go wrong with the sandwich, and he never disappoints."

"Wow," said Parker. "That's a whole lot of information. This is like a dream. How can I help you?"

Hoodsie replied, "I have been out in the field doing research, and I have gathered some important information that I must now report back. Tonight, there is a very important meeting with the whole clan. I have to get back, but I missed the bus."

"What do you mean you missed the bus?" Parker asked.

"Well, I know all the bus routes, and when I need to get back, I just jump on the bus, follow all the lines, then jump onto the next bus until I get back."

"So you need a ride?"

"Yes," said Hoodsie.

"How far do you have to go?"

Hoodsie replied, "It's about a half-hour ride."

"Wow, this still sounds really weird, and it feels like I'm dreaming, but you really sound like you know what you're talking about. Maybe I can help you. I think my friends are still around and haven't left yet. Let me check if they're still here."

Parker ran around the rock and looked down the field. He saw that Paul and Patrick were still talking to some people on the other side of the field. He also noticed that Patti's mom, as well as Patti, were still around.

He told Hoodsie to wait; maybe he could get some help. Parker ran across the field and called out to Patti. When he caught up to her, he then went toward Paul and Patrick and called them over. When they met up, Parker was breathing hard from running across the field to catch them before they left.

Parker then proceeded to tell them the story of his new friend, Hoodsie, knowing how crazy it all sounded but really wanting to help out. He told them bits and pieces about the talking ice cream cup. As expected, they were all really con-fused. Parker sounded serious and believable. As unbelievable as it all sounded, it would have been even more unbelievable for him to have made it all up.

Parker explained that his new friend needed a favor; he needed a ride back to his home. Paul, Patrick, and Patti remained confused as they listened. Parker asked Paul if he could give Hoodsie a ride, explaining that it was about a half-hour away.

Paul, still puzzled, asked Parker, "Where does he live? A house with a family?"

"Well, no, not a house, but yes, he does live with a family," said Parker. "And we all would love his family."

Patti intervened. "What do you mean? How would you know that we would love them? Do you know them?"

Parker replied, "Actually, we already love his family. His family is all the other ice cream novelties, and since we all love ice cream, we already love his family."

"Hoodsie loves ice cream too."

"He does?" asked Patti.

"Yes, of course, he does. Since ice cream novelties are his family, and since he loves his family, he loves ice cream, just like we all do."

Parker explained that Hoodsie didn't live in a house but in a warehouse, where they did very important work.

"Can we do it? Paul, can we give him a ride... please?" Parker pleaded. "He needs to get back right away; he has time-sensitive information to share with his clan—his family."

Patrick, intrigued, said, "Well, we have the time. It's always nice to help someone in need. We can do our good deed for the day."

While all this was going on, Hoodsie was quietly observing

and hoping he could get that ride he was so desperately seeking. Parker introduced Hoodsie to his friends.

Hoodsie noticed Paul and remembered seeing him before. After some thought, he recalled that Paul is the one who told the story of the old antique ice cream truck with the name *Peter Palagi Ice Cream* on it. Hoodsie had overheard the conversation while being stuck under the trash barrel.

Now anxious to get that ride and especially excited that he has run into Paul, Hoodsie asks him for a ride, promising to explain more of his story along the way. Paul considers what Patrick had said—the fact that they had the time and that it always feels good to do a good deed. He agrees and tells everyone to follow him to get the car.

Now living in this new, weird, and unbelievable reality, Paul is beginning to accept that this Hoodsie cup has somehow come to life and is talking. And now, apparently, it needs their help. Paul asks Hoodsie if he knows how to get to his home.

Hoodsie replies, "Yes, we're going towards Taunton, Massachusetts. That's where the home of the New England Ice Cream Corporation is, and that is our home—our *new* home. New England Ice Cream had just opened for business with the plan of spreading happiness all over New England."

"Spreading happiness?" Pattie asks.

"Yes, spreading happiness. That's where we come in. They send us all over New England. When we arrive and when we are chosen, people are happy. We all work together. They need us, and we need them."

Still confused by everything, Pattie responds, "Well... that makes sense... I guess."

They all get in the car and start heading toward Taunton, Massachusetts, under Hoodsie's guidance, telling Paul which way to go.

On their way, Paul and his good friend Patrick embark on another adventure—this time with their new friends, Parker and Pattie, who are also best friends.

Hoodsie, aware of how crazy this all sounds and how confused his new friends must be, begins telling his story. He also mentions his pressing need to get back home.

"You all know how happy you get when you're having ice cream—and sometimes even happier just knowing that you're *going* to get it," Hoodsie says.

Parker and his friends, familiar with that feeling, nod enthusiastically in agreement.

Hoodsie continues, "So, knowing that our purpose is to make people happy, we've been doing research for a long time on why ice cream makes them happy."

"After extensive research, we identified different reasons. We quickly realized that *where* people get ice cream affects the degree of happiness. We came up with five different ways people get ice cream and the level of happiness each delivers."

Hoodsie lays out some of his clan's research, hoping his new friends will better understand their work.

"One way is when people pick up ice cream from a supermarket while grocery shopping. They take it home, put it in their freezer, and at some point—maybe while watching TV—they go over, get some ice cream, and enjoy it. Yeah, pretty cool... but the delay from when they buy it to when they actually have it takes away most of the excitement."

"A second way people get ice cream is from a convenience store. Maybe after getting gas or stepping in for something else, they see an ice cream novelty, and—maybe because they're a little hungry—they grab it as a pick-me-up snack. They eat it in the car as they drive away. It serves a purpose, sure they're happy, but it was just a convenient thing to do. That's why they call them *convenience* stores."

"Another way people get ice cream is at events—maybe after dinner, as dessert. Dessert is always something to look forward to, and it makes people happy. But again, it's more of a 'because it's there' moment."

"The fourth way is when people decide to *go out* for ice cream. The thought of all those flavors and toppings—choosing the perfect combination—is an exciting moment. Plus, the social aspect of going out with friends, relaxing, and enjoying each other's company makes it even more special."

Parker and his friends take in all this information, not quite sure what to make of it, but agree that it kind of makes sense.

Hoodsie continues, "Then there's the *ice cream truck!* Getting ice cream from the ice cream truck has the biggest impact and creates the happiest experience."

"With all our research, we found that the most *impactful* way people get ice cream is when the ice cream truck shows up. It's a thrilling and special moment."

"We believe people get so excited about the ice cream truck because it *comes to them*—sometimes when they least expect it—offering all those great options, sometimes in the most *inconvenient* convenient places."

"Another reason it's exciting is that it's affordable. Most people have at least a few dollars in their pocket, making it easy to grab a treat."

"The arrival of the ice cream truck is a special moment that brings out the child in all of us, sparking childhood memories."

Wrapping up this part of his story, Hoodsie continues, "Since we determined that getting ice cream from an ice cream truck creates the greatest happiness—and with *our* purpose being to make people happy—we set out to find the best representation we could. We wanted to make sure we made the right connections—to be represented by the best."

"So, we started looking for ice cream men who are

*passionate* about their work and whose purpose aligns with ours—to make people happy. They can help us fulfill our purpose, and we can help them fulfill theirs."

Paul comments, "Wow, that's a lot of work... but I get it. If you're passionate about your work, you do everything in your power to get it right. I commend you and your clan."

Paul then brings up his encounter with Peter Palagi. "I ran into this ice cream man whose name was—"

"Peter Palagi!" Hoodsie excitedly interrupts. "I know Peter Palagi!"

Paul, surprised, asks, "Yes... but how do you know?"

"I heard you tell your story before."

Paul, confused, responds, "We just met—how could you have heard me?"

Hoodsie explains, "I was stuck under the trash barrel when you were getting ice cream and telling your story. *Peter Palagi* is the one we've been looking for. And we've been searching for him for a long time."

"You mentioned something about Pawtucket?"

"Yes—Pawtucket, Rhode Island, next to a baseball stadium," Paul confirms.

"I *know!*" Hoodsie exclaims. "This is the closest we've ever been! That's why I need to get back—to report that we have a hot lead. I *think* we've found him!"

Hoodsie then shares some of the terrible experiences he's had while doing field research. "Yes, we make people happy—but we can't do it alone. It's a team effort. A good ice cream man *and* us working together make the experience special. You've probably heard the phrase, 'It's the delivery that makes the difference.'"

"I've had some pretty bad experiences with *not-so-good* ice cream men. A bad attitude? A *horrible* trait. If an ice cream man doesn't greet people with a genuine smile, it's not a good start."

"You can see how seriously I take my job," Hoodsie continues. "A good ice cream man should *care*. If a child is just a little short on money, he should give the kid a break. He can catch up to him later... or not. The point is—he should want the kid to be happy, not sad."

"In our research, we kept hearing the name *Peter Palagi*."

"We heard great things—like that he was America's *first* ice cream man. Not sure if that's a fact, but that's part of our research."

"While it is great to be the first at something, that does not guarantee that someone is any good at what they do. It's what they do after they are 'the first' that makes them great."

"We also heard that he was still in business, so we set out to find him and see for ourselves."

"When I heard Paul mention his name, I knew exactly who he was talking about."

Hoodsie and his clan had really put a lot of effort into this search, gathering a lot of information along the way with the goal of fulfilling their purpose and spreading happiness. He would go on and on when talking about their efforts.

He continues, "What we know about Peter Palagi is that he started his company about 100 years ago after having just emigrated from Italy. And he was still in business. We understand how hard it is to keep a business going, as we have seen many come and go. So, to keep it going for 100 years and then some, there's got to be something great and special about how he went about his business. We can only imagine what a great man he must be, and that's why we've been searching for him for a long, long time. He must have gone about his work with great passion and pride, always striving to fulfill his purpose with great discipline and determination."

"That's the kind of ice cream man we crave to work with, a man who feels a great sense of purpose, which in turn helps us achieve our purpose. We knew we were close, and we had pinpointed his location as being somewhere in the Northeast. In the last few months, we were looking in the state of Massachusetts, and finally, we got some leads that he was in Rhode Island."

"When I got to Lippitt Park in Providence, I knew I was really close. Then I heard Paul tell his story about how he ran into Peter Palagi after a baseball game in Pawtucket, next to a baseball stadium. McCoy Stadium in Pawtucket and Peter Palagi's Ice Cream Company were next to it on Bacon Street."

"I was jumping out of my shell when I heard Paul tell his story," said Hoodsie. "Finally! We were as close as we had ever been to finding Peter Palagi. That's why I needed to get back right away, to report that we had found him!"

"Today is the NEW SEASON PLANNING ASSEMBLY."

Hoodsie was just finishing his story as they were arriving at the warehouse. He continued, "Today is Saturday, and Saturdays at the warehouse are special... special mostly for the fact that on Saturdays, all the humans working there go home early. This is the only time that we are there alone, with no one supervising — a time to have fun and let loose. So, before the big meeting, we will be having recreation."

"What do you mean, recreation?" Patti asked.

Hoodsie responded, "Well, it means that all the ice cream novelties get a chance to loosen up, get out of their neatly packed boxes, run around, and have fun for a few hours after being frozen stiff all week long, waiting to be sent out to fulfill their purpose."

Hoodsie asked everyone in the car if they wanted to go inside. They all looked at each other, and their gestures suggested, well... yeah, of course, this was an opportunity that should not be missed after coming all this way.

"Great, follow me," Hoodsie said.

He then took them to the back door and let them in, leading them to the freezer door. He told them to gear up with the winter clothes hanging just outside the door: heavy jackets, winter hats, gloves, as it is frigid cold inside the walk-in freezer.

He needed to talk to his executive committee and let them know that they had company. He also needed to freshen up and get refilled with ice cream. Actually, he needed to get rid of his old shell (cup) and get a new cup with ice cream. That was the benefit of having immunity — to renew himself and continue the journey of making sure he did his job. It was kind of like taking a shower and putting on clean clothes, and then going back to work.

Hoodsie said, "Wait here outside the freezer until I come back and let you know that everything is okay."

Someone said, "Okay," and some just nodded. As they began to bundle up as if they were going out in the middle of a winter storm, they started making comments about this great new experience. None of them had ever been to an ice cream warehouse before.

Parker and his friends were now the guests — the guests that no one expected... strangers, really. As delighted as they were to be there, they were ecstatic at the thought and the opportunity of going inside the big freezer, kind of like going into a whole new world.

Parker and his friends were on cloud nine. "What a thrill to be here," said Patrick.

Patti agreed, "This is awesome!"

"Ditto," said Parker.

As they were ready to go into the freezer, they didn't

really know what to expect. They imagined that it would be extraordinarily cold, like being in the North Pole, and that there would be a whole bunch of boxes of ice cream novelties neatly stacked on shelves.

Hoodsie came back and told them that everything was okay and they could go in now. Paul took the initiative to pull the door open. It was a huge, heavy door. After opening that door, there was a second door, just as heavy, before getting into the actual massive freezer where the clan lived.

They had forgotten that Hoodsie told them that they would be having recreation, to take advantage of the fact that no one was working at the time and they were unsupervised. This was the only chance they had to have fun and loosen up.

When they opened the second door and went inside, they did not expect what they saw. They were astonished as they saw the scene before them. The place looked like a giant athletic facility with lots of activity. It had turned into a big recreation area, and everyone in the clan was involved in some kind of game or sport. After all, it was recreation time while there were no humans supervising. The ICE CREAM NOVELTIES WERE ALIVE, ALL OF THEM.

By this time, they had accepted the fact that Hoodsie was alive like a person, as they had been having conversations with him. Not one of them had really stopped to think that the others would also be alive. So, here they were, all of them... alive and actively engaged in what appeared to be a sort of sports carnival, separated by sections with different activities at each section. Every different section also had its own music.

On one side, there was a football game going on between the chocolate éclairs (who have a reputation for being the jocks of the family) against the chips galore and the cookies and cream sandwiches, who generally stick together.

On another side, there was a basketball game between the Looney Tunes screamers and the malt cups (on the same team) playing against a few characters that were part of the clan: SpongeBob, Spiderman, Batman, Sonic, and Dora. Looney Tunes and the screamers are the best of friends, always hanging around together.

In another corner of the freezer, the Hoodsie cups had scraped up and gathered all the snowy ice that sometimes accumulates in a big walk-in freezer and made a hill of snow with it. They were sliding down the snowy hill, joined by the crybaby Italian ices, who generally hang out with the Hoodsie cups.

On yet another side were the two-ball screwballs and the nutty-buddies, involved in some kind of erratic game that was hard to figure out. They had probably just made it up, making up their own rules as they went. Well, after all, when you think about it, they were the screwballs and nutty-buddies... and who can figure them out?

Then, there were the coconut, mango, and strawberry cream bars under a bright light, almost pretending that they were in some tropical island, taking in the sun and listening to music.

The guests were just walking around, not really saying anything, but their faces were filled with amazement.

The place was buzzing with activity. The members of the clan were not expecting any humans to be there. As they started seeing the guests, they began to freeze up (stand still). They were under the impression that there were no humans there and didn't want to get caught doing something they were not supposed to be doing. They lived this secret life, and only they knew about it.

Hoodsie, the one who brought them there and was leading them through, noticed everyone freezing up as he passed by with his guests. Then he realized that they were having recreation because his family thought no humans were there. He took the initiative to let them all know what was happening.

"Listen up, everyone, it's okay, these are my new friends," he said loudly so everyone could hear. "They are our guests for today's meeting." Again, he repeated, "It's okay, they know all about us."

There was a sigh of relief, and slowly everyone started moving again. No one wanted to waste any valuable recreation time, as they knew it was very limited. They all believed in a balanced life—work hard, play hard—and this was their time to loosen up and have some fun before having to go back to work.

Hoodsie continued with the tour. On yet another side, they saw creamsicles and fudgicles getting ready for a soccer game.

Patti pointed them out. "Wow, look at them getting ready for a soccer game. That looks like fun!"

Hoodsie responded, "Yes, they're always playing soccer. They're very competitive—cousins against cousins."

Patti asked, "What do you mean, cousins?"

"Yeah, cousins... Dreamsicles and fudge bars, they're cousins," replied Hoodsie.

Parker jumped in, "What... cousins?"

Patrick and Paul were just taking it all in. They had questions but didn't really ask. They were simply enjoying the moment.

Patti, however, had questions and wanted answers. She was curious and confused, so she asked, "Wait... what? They are cousins? Don't you have to have both parents be siblings in order for them to be cousins? You mean the dream bar and the fudge bar have parents? Who are their parents? This is all crazy."

Hoodsie responded, "Well, you know, they're not really cousins... Well, they've been good friends for a long time. At some point, one of their friends referred to them as cousins. Others heard that, and 'cousins' stuck in their minds. Since then, everyone would refer to them as your cousin when mentioning them, so they just went with it. They were cousins who weren't really cousins but were really cousins by circumstance, and they'd been cousins for a long time. Don't you know someone like that? At the end of the day, it really wasn't that important, and nobody really cares, so we'll leave them as cousins. It doesn't change anything."

Parker chimed in, "I'm good with that. I have friends in the same situation. We just go with it."

Hoodsie brought up another situation. "There's also the shortcake and the éclair—they're also related."

Patti jumped in again, still not accepting any of this. "Are they cousins too?"

Hoodsie responded, "No, they're not cousins. They're a couple."

Paul was still just patiently watching, apparently entertained by it all.

Patti was still struggling with this whole concept. "What?! A couple? This is all just too much."

Hoodsie responded, "Well, they're always together and they get along great. Everyone assumes they're a couple. Strawberry and chocolate are kind of opposites, but you know, sometimes opposites attract. Sometimes you do hear them bickering about what's better—chocolate or strawberry—but they're a couple, and everyone knows it."

Parker again chimed in, "It's their thing. Let them be a couple; it doesn't change a thing. Good for them."

Patrick, who had been quiet and just observing, like Paul, and apparently enjoying this circus (well, sort of a circus), remarked, "Wow, this has been quite a tour! I can't wait for the assembly. Maybe there will be more surprises."

It was getting close to the end of recreation time, and it was time to get ready for "The Annual Assembly Meeting." Hoodsie needed to meet with the executive board to prepare for the meeting. He told Parker and his friends to make themselves at home, and if they got cold, to just step out of the freezer and warm up a bit.

No doubt, they were cold. They started heading toward the door. On the way out, Paul noticed a sign, but he couldn't make out what it said as it had built up ice on most of it. The only thing he could make out was the letter P, then some letters that were covered by ice, followed by another P. Paul didn't think much of it, just that it kind of rang a bell, something he had seen before. He went back outside the freezer to warm up before going back in for the assembly, where a big announcement was supposed to be made.

To start settling everyone down and get them ready, it was Mr. Ice Cream Sandwich's job to make sure everyone would settle down and begin to prepare. The clan was settling down and getting ready for the meeting.

As Parker and his friends were just outside the freezer warming up before going back in for the meeting, they started talking about what they had just witnessed inside the walk-in freezer.

Patti said, "That was awesome!"

Patrick agreed, "Yeah, pretty awesome."

Paul asked the group, "Did anyone see the sign inside the freezer near the door?"

They all acknowledged that they saw it, mostly by nodding, with some saying yes.

Parker commented, "How could we not see it? It was too

big to miss, and in the perfect spot—you'd have to be blind to miss it."

Eyes wide open and nodding in agreement, they all seemed to be on the same page about the sign.

Now that everyone acknowledged they saw it, Paul was curious and asked, "Could anyone make out what it said?"

A couple of comments were made, and they all seemed to suggest the same thing—they could only see the two Ps and didn't think much of it.

Hoodsie came back out of the freezer to check on his friends and let them know that the assembly was about to begin. He told them they were special guests and he wanted them to be part of the meeting. They all looked at each other, and Patrick said, "Well, we're already here, so we might as well experience everything about your clan."

They bundled up and headed back inside the freezer. Everything had changed. Earlier, when they had been inside before stepping out, the whole place was a big recreation center with lots of activity. Now, everyone was orderly and ready for the executive committee to come out and announce the plans for the new season.

In front of the room, there was a long table with 10 chairs for the executive board. The Choco Taco sat in the middle. He was the leader—a wise, well-respected member of the clan. He had a powerful, commanding voice, similar to the Wizard in *The Wizard of Oz*.

Parker and his friends went back inside to attend the meeting as special guests. When they entered, it was like night and day compared to before. Everyone was orderly and neatly lined up, ready to pay attention to what Mr. Choco Taco had to say and to hear about the new plans for the season.

# THE MEETING BEGINS

M r. Choco Taco began bringing the meeting to order.
"Good afternoon, everyone, including our guests. Here we are again, at the beginning of yet another ice cream season. We will continue working with our already existing customers and nurturing those relationships, while looking for new opportunities to extend our reach and expand on our purpose."

"As you all know, our purpose is to make people happy. Every year, we review our progress in that research to continue achieving our main goal and purpose. The main conclusion our research has led us to is that people are happiest when we come out of an ice cream truck."

"An ice cream truck does not work alone; it needs an ice cream man. Naturally, those have been the connections we have been searching for. We set out to find an ice cream man who was aligned with our purpose and passionate about his work. Through the grapevine of our research, we kept hearing the name Peter Palagi."

"From bits and pieces of his story that we've been able to put together, as far as we know, it appears that Peter Palagi was the first ice cream man. Not just the ice cream man, but a businessman running his own ice cream business. And here we are, 100 years later, his ice cream business is still in business today."

"We've been on a mission to find Peter Palagi."

"I know this Peter Palagi character sounds like a folktale, but if it turns out that everything we've heard is true, and he's real, he seems to be aligned with our beliefs. Passion and purpose must drive him. He must love what he does."

Mr. Choco Taco continued, "Today, I have some great and exciting news for you." Everyone was anxious to hear.

"We have some special guests here today: Parker, Patti, Patrick, and Paul. Parker and Patti are best friends, and Patrick and Paul are also best friends and have been for a lifetime. They're all ice cream lovers, just like us."

"Hoodsie, who we all know and is on our Executive Board, was out on the field doing research when he overheard a story Paul told about the day he ran into an ice cream truck. The truck had the name 'Peter Palagi Ice Cream' on it. And the person in the truck happened to be Peter Palagi himself."

"The story of Peter Palagi almost sounded too good to be true, but no—Peter is not only real, but he's alive and well!"

"Our special guests know where Peter is! They will lead us to him."

Upon hearing the news, there was a buzz of excitement in the air as everyone in the clan knew how important this was. This was great news.

Just as Mr. Choco Taco was speaking, he noticed the sign hanging by the door. You could only see two "P"s due to the ice build-up covering the rest of the letters. Mr. Choco Taco asked if someone could go over to the sign and brush the ice off so that it would be visible to everyone. The sign displayed the motto of the clan.

Mr. Ice Cream Sandwich grabbed a broom and brushed off the ice that was covering the rest of the sign. Parker and his friends were very curious to see what the sign said. As the ice that had accumulated on it was brushed off, the sign was finally revealed. It read "PASSION & PURPOSE." Now they could see what the two "P"s stood for.

"Thank you," said Mr. Choco Taco, then continued to speak. He read the sign and started from there. "Passion and Purpose— that sign is up there to remind us all why we are here. We are passionate about the work that we do, which leads us to fulfill our purpose. Passion is about pursuing the things that make us happy, while purpose is using our unique talents and passions to make others happy. All of us here have the same purpose: to make people happy."

It was due to Hoodsie's great work and diligence that the answers they had been seeking for so long were finally found. Everyone in the clan was excited about the news and congratulated Hoodsie for his triumph in finding Peter Palagi and his great investigative work. He had put in a lot of time in the field, often in uncomfortable situations.

As everyone celebrated the great news, Patti was looking at the sign with the double "P"s. She saw something strange and weirdly familiar about the sign... almost convinced that she had seen it before, but she couldn't quite figure it out. There's something about that sign, she thought, something different and special...

Then something clicked in her mind. She was in deep thought for a minute or so... then... BINGO! She realized that the "P P" they had originally seen were the initials for Peter Palagi, the same as the first two letters of "PASSION" and "PURPOSE." She wondered if that was just a coincidence, as if Peter Palagi had something to do with "PASSION" and "PURPOSE." Maybe that was the connection, and no one really knew. They both needed each other: Peter needed the members of the clan, and they needed Peter Palagi to deliver those magic moments that they both felt was their ultimate goal— to make people happy.

Still believing that it might just be a coincidence, she thought it was all great, but still believed there was more to that sign. She couldn't figure it out.

"What else is it about that sign?" she asked herself. She thought... hmmm... looking at the sign some more... then she thought of something. Her name began with a "P"— Patti. Then she realized, so did her last name— Pine. She thought, *Well, that can't be it. That's just another coincidence.*

She called Parker over to tell him about the sign, hoping he could help connect some dots. After calling Parker, she realized that Parker's name also began with a "P." Then she thought... wait a minute... Parker's last name is Perry, which also starts with a "P."

She thought... Hmmm... that's a little weird.

She told Parker the story about the sign and all the connections. He also thought it was just a coincidence, but then he paused for a second... then he said, "Wait a minute, Patrick and Paul also begin with a P."

Patti said, "Wow, that's right."

She asked him, "Do you know their last names?"

Parker said, "No, let's ask them." He called them over.

As they approached, Parker asked, "What are your last names?"

Patrick responded, "My last name is Powers... is everything okay?"

Paul said his last name right after Patrick, "My last name is Peterson."

Patti and Parker were speechless, their mouths wide open.

Paul also asked, "Is everything okay?"

Patti and Parker were still speechless...

Patrick asked again, "Is everything okay? Why do you ask about our last names?"

Patti said, "This can't be a coincidence..." Shocked by the

revelation, she went on to tell Paul and Patrick the story about the sign and the fact that the "PASSION and PURPOSE" sign shared the same "P P" as in Peter Palagi...

Paul said, "Hmmm, what a coincidence."

"That's what I thought," said Patti. "I thought it was a coincidence too... at first. But then my name also has those initials..."

Patrick and Paul didn't think it was a big deal but felt there was more to the story.

Patti continued, "But wait, there's more..." "My name is Patti, and my last name is Pine. Then I called Parker over and realized that Parker's last name was Perry. Then we called you guys over and you're Paul Peterson and Patrick's last name is Powers."

Now it was Patrick and Paul's turn to be caught with their mouths wide open.

Paul, being the most philosophical one of the bunch, said, "That's no coincidence. Sometimes things happen for a reason, and sometimes you never even figure out what the reason is."

But here, he felt certain that all these things happened for a reason. He summarized everything that had happened: "The fact that we all met, my experience of running into Peter Palagi some 20-something years ago, us meeting you kids, and all of us ending up going to the ice cream warehouse to meet the clan who uses a motto of 'Passion and Purpose,' two words that start with the letter 'P,' which are the same initials as Peter Palagi, as well as the same initials of all of us... and we all ended up here, as we had something that they needed— information on the whereabouts of Peter Palagi. That's exactly what they were looking for... all that was no coincidence. I believe all this was supposed to happen... like destiny."

Mr. Choco Taco was starting to wrap up the meeting.

With the great news of finding out where Peter Palagi was and the thought that they would go meet him, everyone was excited and optimistic that it would be a great summer.

He asked his guests, "Will you be heading back to Providence?" as he knew that's where they came from. He also knew that it wasn't far from Pawtucket.

Paul responded, "Yes."

Mr. Taco then asked, "Will you take me and a few members of the board to Peter Palagi's Ice Cream Company headquarters in Pawtucket?"

Paul, who was the one driving, said, "Yes, not a problem."

As the meeting wrapped up, Choco Taco was gathering his executive board and telling them about his plan to head out to see Peter Palagi. They all got in the car and headed toward Pawtucket.

As they got closer, they saw the baseball stadium, the famous McCoy Stadium. All the memories of that great night were coming back, the night they met Peter Palagi.

Paul never forgot the name of the street— Bacon Street. He remembered making the comment, "Ice cream on Bacon Street," two things he really liked. That always stuck in his mind.

There was excitement in the air as everyone knew they were close. They drove by the stadium and continued looking for Bacon Street. The first street after the stadium was Bacon Street, Paul remembered. They made a right turn and headed down the street. About halfway down, they arrived.

They pulled into the lot, but it appeared that no one was there. The garage doors were wide open. Looking inside, they saw an old antique ice cream truck with peeling paint. You could still make out the name "Peter Palagi Ice Cream" on it. When Patrick and Paul saw it, they recognized it. That was

Peter's truck that they had gotten ice cream from some 25 years prior— an exciting moment for them for sure.

Parker was excited that all this was happening, while also beginning to feel a little tired. He went back outside to the parking lot, squinted his eyes, and felt like he wanted to take a nap. He looked up at the sun... then he heard someone call his name, "Parker!" He actually heard other voices calling his name too.

Parker turned, and he was no longer in the lot at the company headquarters. He was behind the rock at the playground where he had been playing with Patti earlier that day. He started to look to see who was calling his name, so he went around the rock and saw a police officer calling for him.

Parker said, "Hi, I'm Parker."

The police officer ran over to him and asked, "Are you okay?"

Parker said, "Yes, of course I'm all right. Why wouldn't I be?"

The police officer announced, "He's here! I found him behind the rock!"

Parker asked, "What?"

The police officer told him that they had been looking for him and thought he might be lost.

In the meantime, Parker's grandfather approached him, along with all the other people helping to look for him. Apparently, Parker had sat down behind the rock, and since he was tired from all the running around, he had fallen asleep on the shady side. As the sun had started to hit his face, he woke up.

He realized that his whole trip— the ice cream warehouse and meeting Hoodsie— was a dream, but it all seemed too real. He couldn't believe it was just a dream. Parker's grandfather came over and gave him a great big hug and was relieved that he was okay. Parker began to tell Grandpa about his dream, still believing that it was real.

Parker had a reputation for telling stories, so Grandpa didn't mind, but he knew it was just a dream. He was just relieved that Parker was okay.

Parker asked his grandpa if he could take him to the ice cream company that Paul had talked about. He remembered that it was behind the baseball stadium in Pawtucket and also remembered Bacon Street. Grandpa figured it wasn't that far and agreed to take him, so off they went.

When they got to Bacon Street, they didn't have an exact address, but Parker did remember Bacon Street. They drove down the street, hoping they would just see it. The street wasn't long, and about midway down, they came to a lot that had one ice cream truck parked inside of it. On the front door, there was a sign that read, "Palagis Ice Cream Company." Parker figured that this must be the place. It was missing Peter's name, but "Palagi" was part of the name.

This lot didn't look like the one in his dream, and at that point, Parker accepted that it had been a dream when he fell asleep. Even though his dream felt so real, he thought, "Well, this is even better. This is the real thing."

They drove into the lot, and just like in the dream, the garage doors were wide open, but no one was in sight. They started looking around to see if there was anyone there, then they saw the old truck that Patrick had talked about: an antique ice cream truck in need of a paint job and some attention. You could still see the name "Peter Palagi Ice Cream" on it, which was an exciting moment as they realized they were in the right place. Then a man came out to greet them.

He asked, "Can I help you?"

Parker proceeded to ask the man, "We're here looking for

Peter. Is Peter here? We wanted to meet him, so... is he still around?"

The man answered, "No, Peter is no longer here, but that was his truck, and he sold ice cream from that truck."

"What is your name, young man?"

"My name is Parker, and this is my grandpa."

"Well... he's around, but he no longer works here. He lives nearby."

"Who are you? Are you his son?" asked Parker.

"No, I'm not his son. My name is Alex, and I work here... I'm actually the new owner."

Parker, being a curious young man, had questions. "Is it true that he was the ice cream man for a long... long time? Like 100 years? Was he the first ice cream man?"

"You're a curious young man... and persistent. Both good traits," Alex said.

He continued, "Yes, no, not quite, and sort of. Three questions, three answers: Yes, he was the ice cream man for a long time. The Peter who worked here with me was Peter Palagi Junior, and he was the ice cream man for about 40 years. His father, also named Peter Palagi Senior, was the ice cream man for another 40 years or so. They were both named Peter Palagi, so Peter Palagi was the ice cream man for about 80 years. And yes, he was the first ice cream man, but it was Peter Palagi Senior first, and then his son, Peter Palagi Jr., continued the tradition. Nevertheless, Peter Palagi was the first ice cream man."

"There was actually a fleet of six of those trucks, and they all had the name 'Peter Palagi Ice Cream' on them."

Then he went on to tell Parker and his grandpa that he was the new owner of the ice cream company.

"I know you came in looking for Peter Palagi. He's not here... but it's almost as if he is, in me. My name is not Peter

Palagi. My name is Alex, and I run the company now. I run it with the same passion and pride that Peter did, and with the same mutual purpose, which is to make people happy. This company was built on hard work, discipline, and dedication, and it has stood the test of time on those same principles. It continues to do so because all those principles have been passed down from generation to generation to generation, and now also to me. So, Peter is kind of still here, in me."

Parker and his grandpa were elated with everything they learned about Peter Palagi, the first ice cream man. They were also very appreciative of the new owner, Alex, who took his time to show them around and share all the information about the ice cream company—quite a history, they thought.

Realizing that it had been a long day and it was getting late, Parker asked Alex if it was okay for him to visit again and bring some friends.

Alex told him, "Of course it's okay, anytime."

Parker was happy to hear that and thanked Alex for sharing the history. He said goodbye and left, thrilled with all he had learned about Peter Palagi and the history of Palagis Ice Cream Company. He couldn't wait to tell his good friend Patti all about it.

# EPILOGUE

## INTENTIONS FOR WRITING THIS STORY

My main intention in writing this story was to inform people about the history of this company, which so many hold dear to their hearts, while also placing Peter Palagi in his rightful place in the history books. This is a story told from the inside.

Regardless of the company's long life, a historical account alone might not be very long—or particularly engaging—so, to add color and bring it to life, I infused my own personal touch. My goal was to entertain, inspire, and educate while informing the public about the history of this iconic Pawtucket business. To inform, to inspire, to entertain, and to educate—these are the intentions and the purpose I hope to achieve.

Pawtucket, Rhode Island, is best known as the birthplace of the Industrial Revolution. However, it is not known for being the home of the first ice cream man or the birthplace of the ice cream truck—**it ought to be!** Pawtucket resident Pietro (Peter) Palagi Sr., who founded the Peter Palagi Ice Cream Company in 1896, became the first ice cream man in America. Through his work and innovations, he also became known as "The Father of the Ice Cream Truck."

We live in an extraordinary time, with information on any topic at our fingertips, thanks to the invention of the smartphone—now owned by 98% of the U.S. population. It has almost become a body part as you wouldn't leave home without it.

Yet, if you do a Google search on your smartphone for the first ice cream truck, the result credits Harry Burt of Youngstown, Ohio, with its invention in 1920. Burt was the creator of the Good Humor brand.

Knowing what I know, I reached out to the Ohio Historical Preservation office—the source of that information—to tell them about Peter Palagi of Pawtucket, Rhode Island. Peter had been selling ice cream from a horse-drawn wagon *at least* 20 years before 1920, the date attributed to the first ice cream truck. I wanted to make it clear that long before Ohio's Harry Burt put a freezer on a truck and began selling ice cream, Peter Palagi was already vending ice cream on the streets—just with a horse and wagon instead of a motorized vehicle.

The difference, perhaps, lies in the fact that in 1920, Harry Burt's trucks were motorized, officially making them "trucks" rather than horse-drawn wagons. However, when discussing the history of the ice cream truck—and, more specifically, the first ice cream truck—Peter Palagi's story should be front and center in that conversation.

Peter's innovations in horse-and-wagon ice cream vending laid the groundwork for the first ice cream trucks. Additionally, when searching for information about the first ice cream truck on Google, related questions appear—including one asking, "Who was the first ice cream man?" The answer? Google states that it's unknown, speculating that it was probably one of Harry Burt's employees.

But we know that Harry Burt's refrigerated trucks debuted in 1920. That means any of his employees wouldn't have started selling ice cream until at the earliest, 1920—perhaps for a week, a month, or even a season or two.

So, let's set the record straight: Peter Palagi Sr. was selling ice cream at least 20 years before Harry Burt's trucks even existed.

Peter Palagi Sr. was the first ice cream man. He was in the ice cream business for about 40 years, and as if that wasn't enough, his son, Peter Palagi Jr., continued the business for at least another 40 years. For roughly 80 years, refrigerated trucks roamed the streets of Pawtucket, Rhode Island, and surrounding communities, proudly displaying the name Peter Palagi Ice Cream. This cemented the legacy of "Peter Palagi, The Ice Cream Man" in Pawtucket's local history, in the history of Rhode Island, and in the history of America.

Unfortunately, this history remains largely unknown outside of Rhode Island and parts of Massachusetts—for now. I hope to change that with this book.

It almost sounds like a myth, a legend—but Peter Palagi was real. The business he started over 125 years ago is still operating today, and I hope to spread his story beyond Rhode Island's borders. Just as an ice cream truck draws people toward it upon arrival, this book—the story of America's first ice cream man—has the potential to captivate children and adults alike. For many, the idea of the ice cream truck and the ice cream man is already a cherished part of childhood, making this a story worth telling and remembering.

The Ohio Historical Society found my story compelling and interesting, but they could not add it to their history because they only published Ohio history.

I'm not interested in adding Peter Palagi's story to the history of Ohio, but rather in placing his story where it truly belongs. It belongs in the history of America—Peter Palagi, the first ice cream man and the father of the ice cream truck.

While doing my due diligence and continuing my research, I also visited the Rhode Island Historical Society. There, I was greeted by a woman whom I believe was in charge. I told her the story of this famous Rhode Islander, Peter Palagi, and I also shared my Google search results regarding the first ice cream truck and the first ice cream man—how the story that comes up is that of Harry Burt from Ohio. She was intrigued.

She laughed and, with a grin, proceeded to ask me, "So you want to change history?"

Not expecting that question, I said, "Well, yeah." Then, after thinking about my answer for a few seconds, I added, "Well, I don't want to change history—the history has already been made—I just want to get it right." She thought it was a great story, but she told me there wasn't anything she could do, as that was not what they did.

I also reached out to the Pawtucket Historical Society, and I got the same response—they couldn't do anything.

These experiences really motivated me to push forward, write this story, and attempt to set the record straight. Maybe, if I do a good job, Peter's story will get some well-deserved attention and eventually catch the attention of Google. This was my best idea for spreading awareness of Peter Palagi's story well beyond Pawtucket and Rhode Island's borders.

## TO ENTERTAIN

***Hoodsie's Story:*** Believe it or not, the basic idea for this story was written over twenty-five years ago. And yes, maybe it was just a cute little story that I dreamt up, but at the time, it didn't seem like enough for more than just that—a cute little story.

About a year ago, I was out having dinner with my younger sister Luz. She and I are the babies of the family—the youngest boy and youngest girl of eight siblings. She made a comment about Palagis Ice Cream Company, saying that the story should be told.

I told her that I already had it—well, sort of—and I shared with her the story of Hoodsie and his family that I had written some 25-plus years ago. It was a story about ice cream coming to life and searching for Peter.

My sister, having written a book herself, *Morphing in Stillness*, was very excited and entertained by the story—she couldn't get enough. We even had to schedule another lunch date just to finish discussing it. My sister was right—the story ought to be told.

I had always believed that, eventually, I would write it. And now, after running the company for 25 years, I was in a different mindset—it was time. Combining the story of Hoodsie and his family with the history of the company was something I believed I could find a way to do—to inform and entertain.

## TO EDUCATE

I feel that, naturally, I tend to be a teacher. I enjoy sharing lessons from my experiences whenever the opportunity arises, always with the good intention that someone may benefit from a lesson that serves them. As I consider writing a book—one that will likely attract a young audience—I see an extraordinary opportunity to pass on some of the great lessons I've been fortunate to learn.

I believe in the quote, "You live, you learn, and you pass it on" (H. Jackson Brown). Knowledge gained from experience holds immense value, and taking those lessons to the grave is not only a waste but also a selfish act. I encourage others to share their knowledge and experiences—it costs nothing, yet it may change a life. My goal is to *entertain, inform, and educate.*

## TO INSPIRE—*THE VEGETABLES IN THE SOUP*

Some of you, the adults in the room, may remember being told as children, "Make sure you eat your vegetables; they will make you big, strong, and healthy when you grow up." If you liked vegetables, that sounded great. But if you didn't, it almost felt like a trick. Especially when Mom added that eating your vegetables would not only help you grow big and strong but also make you smart! What pressure for a child—just eat the vegetables!

Even though it may have seemed like a trick, the idea sparked something in your mind. You believed that if you ate your vegetables, you would grow up to be big, strong, and now—smart too. That thought alone made you give those vegetables a chance. But then reality set in—the moment arrived to actually eat them. I was one of those kids who didn't like vegetables—and, unfortunately, I still don't. It was a tough sell for me, but I tried. I really made the effort.

Moms would do anything to get their children to eat vegetables, even hiding them in food if necessary. If they could sneak vegetables into ice cream and make kids fall for it, they would! I am no longer responsible for feeding the children, so I don't have to make soup packed with vegetables.

However, I now have the opportunity to pack my book with "vegetables" of a different kind. I am betting that children reading this book will eagerly consume them—nourishing their souls, encouraging positivity, and motivating them to dream big and accomplish great things.

The "vegetables" in this book are positive thoughts, inspiring quotes, and stories that instill valuable life lessons.

"If you plant a seed in the mind of a child, as they grow, the seed grows with them and eventually becomes a part of them—a seed of positivity with a dose of life's great lessons."          *—AA*

At the end of the day, the hope is that children will be drawn to this book primarily because of its subject matter—one of their favorite things—ice cream and the ice cream truck. As they enjoy the story, they will also take in the "vegetables" within the book—valuable lessons and positive messages—that will hopefully have a lasting impact on their young minds. The goal is for them to grow not just physically strong, but to develop strong, inspired minds filled with big dreams... and yes, to become smart, too.

## THE VEGETABLES IN THE BOOK

"You can't go back to the beginning but start where you are and change the end."
          *—James R. Sherman*

"You live, you learn, and you pass it on."
          *—H. Jackson Brown, Jr. (author)*

"There is a lot more to learn from one tough loss than from twenty great victories."
          *—Alejandro Arteaga (AA)*

"Instead of buying your kids everything that you never had teach them everything that you were never taught. Material things wear out but knowledge stays."          *—Bruce Lee*

"The foundation of an educated man is one who is curious and well read, has good manners and empathy for people, as well as able to adapt to different situations."     —*AA*

"Appreciate everything and say *thank you* often when appropriate. *"Thank You"*: the two most powerful words in the English language.

—*AA*

"Everything as well as everyone fills a purpose, they all fit in somewhere and make a difference."

—*AA*

"My story doesn't end when I die, it continues through my children and those people who knew me and the ones who loved me."     —*AA*

"See the world as a place with unlimited possibilities."     —*AA*

"Connect with others and build and nurture relationships."     —*AA*

"*Passion* is about pursuing the things that make us happy, while *purpose* is using your unique talents and passions to make others happy."

"MBA (Mop Bucket Attitude): the willingness to do whatever it takes to get the job done, the belief that no job is beneath you, and all work is honorable."     —*Dave Thomas*

"In the middle of every difficulty lies opportunity."
—*Albert Einstein*

"A CEO one ought to lead by example. If a leader is not willing to do something himself then he should not ask his employees to do it. A leader should be the biggest team player, coach, and cheerleader and let everyone know that we're all in this together." —*Dave Thomas*

"That which does not kill you will only make you stronger." —*Friedrich Nietzsche*

"Running a business is not all sunshine and roses.
"Running a business is not for the faint of heart, it's for the brave, the patient and persistent. It's for the overcomer."

"The team is priority, our community is our team, think community first and we all win.
—*AA*

"What benefits the community benefits us."
—*AA*

"When one door closes, five windows open up"
—*AA*

"The journey of a thousand miles begins with one single step." —*Lao Tzu, and I add to that,* "That first step is the most important and often the most difficult one." —*AA*

"Easier said than done.

"The best way to get started is to quit talking
and start doing"                    —*Walt Disney*

"If you plant a seed in the mind of a child, as the
child grows the seed grows with them and eventually it becomes them, a seed of positivity and
seeds of life's great lessons."                    —*AA*

"Give yourself permission to be silly, you never
know what wonderfully silly thing you'll come
up with."                                        —*AA*

## TO EDUCATE AND INSPIRE A POSITIVE ATTITUDE

A couple of my intentions in writing this story were to
educate and inspire. I wanted to fully take advantage of this
opportunity, as I may have the attention of many children.
The lessons I present are related to and relevant to the story.
This story has also been about running a business—the dedication required and the struggle to make it all work. One of
the things that helps with getting through the daily grind of
work and the management of a business is maintaining a positive attitude and thinking positive thoughts. Learn positivity,
practice it, and apply it to all aspects of daily life.

Since we're on this *Passion* and *Purpose* journey—two
words that start with "P"—I'm going to take this opportunity
to lay out some positive words that start with "P." I want to
plant a seed in the mind of a child—a seed of positive thoughts
and positivity—with the hope that it will grow as the child
grows and become a part of who they are. Here are some positive "P" words:

*Patience, Persistence, Perseverance, Passionate, Positive, Productive, Profound, Pioneering, Peaceful, Prosperous, Powerful, Polite, Practical, Proud, Perceptive, Persuasive, Phenomenal, Pivotal, Progress, Progressive, Presence, Present, Priority.*

These aren't just words; they are positive words that create a positive mindset. They represent actions and attitudes that not only help in the daily grind of running a business but also help with getting through the struggles of life and the daily challenges we face. I encourage you to read them, learn them, practice them, use them, and allow them to become a part of who you are—a person who sees good, positive things in all situations. I guarantee that life will be better if you allow these words to shape who you are.

If this list ignites a desire in you to read more positive words to aid in growing and maintaining a positive attitude, I urge you to take the initiative and go through the alphabet, from A to Z, writing down all the positive words that start with each letter. Every letter has some! This is such an easy task in this day and age, as we all carry a dictionary and an encyclopedia in our pockets. Children reading this book may not even know what an encyclopedia is, but our modern-day encyclopedia is called a cell phone, and all you have to do is ask whatever you want to know. This simple, fun exercise will benefit you tenfold—ten times the effort you put in. I urge you to be curious.

I'll get you started. It's up to you to do the rest.

A – Amazing, Awesome, Accomplished, Admirable, Approachable, Amiable...

B – Brilliant, Brave, Beautiful, Beneficent, Breathtaking...
C – Cheerful, Clever, Creative, Confident, Curious...
D – Dazzling, Delightful...?
E – ...?
F – ...?

# AUTHOR'S REFLECTIONS

So, you want to write a book? I did. Well, it wasn't really so much about the idea of writing a book, but the telling of a story—a story of a company that's touched so many lives on a local level over the course of the last 125 years. You get the urge to tell a story when you feel that there is an audience who would be interested in hearing it. In my experience, there is quite a bit of interest in what happens on the inside of this company on a daily basis, mainly due to the topic at hand, which is "Ice Cream," and a company involved with ice cream for over a century. There is a certain amount of fascination when it comes to ice cream.

One thing is to tell a story, and another is to write a story... and then there is the publishing of a book—that is a whole other level. I had no idea how much work and time it would take. At the end of the day, it is without a doubt a worthwhile endeavor—something to be proud of, no regrets. The regret would have been not having taken that crucial first step and not having followed through.

I encourage anyone who has a story to tell to just do it. It all begins with that difficult first step, then commit and push through.

Throughout this process of writing this story, intending to hopefully publish it (which is a first for me), there were times when I wondered if this was good enough, entertaining enough, long enough, smart enough—and sometimes the thought crossed my mind that people might think it's just plain silly, second-guessing myself.

Whenever I had those thoughts, I would always think of a story I once heard... a story about a sponge that lived at the bottom of the ocean... inside a pineapple. Pretty silly, right? The sponge had a job as a fry cook. Since he had a job, he wore pants, and since he was a sponge, he was square, so his pants fit square. His name was Bob... yeah, pretty silly. Even sillier than that, they decided to call him "SpongeBob SquarePants." Go figure.

Well, let me tell you, this silly story of SpongeBob SquarePants became the most successful animated series of all time. The thought of that silly story compared to mine led me to believe that my story may not be so silly after all... and then I would get back on track and keep going.

There's a lesson here: you should give yourself permission to be silly. You never know what wonderfully silly thing you may come up with.

By the way, SpongeBob SquarePants is one of the top-selling ice cream popsicles off the ice cream trucks... I would know. SpongeBob has done quite well for himself.

**If the popsicles could talk, what would they say?** The idea for the story of Hoodsie and his family was inspired by the work that we do—that of being an ice cream man. I started working at Palagis Ice Cream Company a few years after high school. As we all look for something to do for work, this is what I ended up doing.

At first, it was just a job—something to do for the summer. I quickly realized that it was more than just a job; it was a business. A business that required a big commitment of time, discipline, and sacrifice in order to make it work. Nothing new here, really. All occupations and businesses require much of the same things in order to be successful.

No experience was needed to run this business—just a driver's license, the commitment of time, and the discipline to stick with it. Very basic stuff, something they call "soft skills," which are things that are crucial to not only getting the job but keeping the job and growing in that job. Some of these things include showing up when you're supposed to, but not just showing up—showing up on time, rested, and ready to work, and bringing a good attitude. Simple skills—those are called soft skills. As simple as these things are, some people are simply not able to keep up with the basic requirements to be successful.

Having started this journey in the new business, I realized that the better I did this, the better off I would be. More soft skills are required in order to build this new business that I had taken on. Some of those include keeping a clean truck, keeping yourself clean and well-groomed, and having a pleasant and friendly demeanor.

Since this is a business, there are always other people trying their hand at it, encroaching on your area—"the competition." I always thought the competition was great for me, as it kept me on my toes and striving to be the best I could be, every day.

I would always notice flaws in the competition, such as a bad attitude, an unclean truck, an unkempt person, high prices, etc.

*If the popsicles could talk, what would they say?* So here I was, new to the business world, realizing that every little bit of business counts and could make the difference between making it or not making it. I made sure to do all the little things that make a big difference in maximizing my opportunity, knowing that there would be others trying to take business away from me.

Knowing there were competitors in my area and being

aware of some of their flaws, I often thought that I always wanted to be the best choice when people had to decide who to do business with—me or a competitor. I consistently did all the little things to ensure I would be the favorite.

I cared very much about that. While working and opening the freezer covers, I would see all these popsicles inside the freezer. One day, I started thinking that if the popsicles had a choice of who to work with, they would want to work with me, mainly because I took great pride in my work and did all the little things to make customers happy.

So, what might the popsicles say if they could talk? They might say something like, "We all know how happy people are when they choose us and we're doing our job. We cannot do this alone. We need help. We need to be well-represented, and we need to find a partner who is willing to do all the little important things required to deliver the happiness that we set out to deliver—our purpose. A partner must have great pride and feel that his purpose is the same as ours—to make people feel happy."

I thought that's what they might say. I needed them, and they needed me—we became a team. Selling sandwiches or anything else just wouldn't have the same effect on people.

# ABOUT THE AUTHOR, ALEJANDRO ARTEAGA

I came to the USA from my native Colombia in the summer of 1976, I was a month away from my tenth birthday. A couple of years after arriving I took on a paper route when I heard from a friend, amongst the group of friends that we would hang out with and play soccer, that he was giving up his paper route. He was a few years older and it was time for him to move on to a bigger and better job. I saw the opportunity and I said, "I'll do it" without hesitation.

At an early age I learned the great satisfaction of work and the great responsibility of my promise. Getting a job is a two way promise, your promise to show up on time and do the work that was asked of you and their promise to pay you a certain amount for your work and your time. I quickly learned that my word, my promise had to be as good as gold, if you gave your word and people expected you to do what you committed to do you could not dare let them down. I took great pride in that job (paper route) and I credit it as an important experience that shaped me at that early age. I had about 90 Pawtucket Times newspapers and about a dozen Providence

Journals to be delivered 6 days a week, rain shine snow ice cold hot flat tire on my bike, it had to be done, no excuses.

I often thought that if you put that kind of responsibility on a young man, one of two things will happen, he'll either sink or he will swim, if he sinks all hope is not lost, he'll have more opportunities to redeem himself, if he swims you'll most likely never have to worry about him.

I think it's unfortunate that paper routes are no longer an option for young kids; it was without a doubt a great character building experience.

Another experience that helped shape me was having access to the Boys and Girls Club of Cumberland Lincoln, The place where I got my first job, after my paper route of course. A place where I played sports in the leagues then moved on to coaching and eventually refereeing, the athlete (the student), the coach (the teacher), the referee (the judge), a full circle education, in my opinion.

I started working at Palagis Ice Cream when I was 20 years old selling ice cream, the job of the ice cream man. I quickly realized that this was not just a job but actually a business, the difference between the two is that a job limits you to an hourly wage and compensation, in a business your compensation was based on your effort and abilities. You could work as many hours as you wanted to and try to be as efficient as you could be in an attempt to be more profit-able, not everybody makes it but some thrive in that kind of environment. Job versus business, I really liked the idea of business, regardless of the uncertainty of that option at times.

Much like Peter Senior 125 years prior where he tried his hand in different businesses, I too tried my hand in different businesses. I started a sporting goods/team uniform store, tried some vending machines and a few others until I came to the conclusion that instead of dividing my % of effort and attention to more than one business I would be more effective if I concentrated 100% of my energy and efforts to one business. That's when I decided that I would pursue the ice cream business. At that time I mentioned to Donald Palagi that I knew the time would come that he would want to retire and that I was interested in taking it over when that time would come, I told him to keep me in mind.

The rest as they say is history.....

# ICE CREAM TRUCKS
## FOR ALL
## OCCASIONS!!!

## REQUEST A TRUCK
### 3 EASY STEPS!

1. Go to: palagisicecream.com
2. Fill Out Truck Request Form
3. Press Send

# WHAT'S YOUR OCCASION?

# WARNING!

## ICE CREAM TRUCK ON THE STREET!!

When you see an **ICE CREAM TRUCK**

On the street

Please **SLOW DOWN** and be aware

that **CHILDREN**

May be **CROSSING** the **STREET**

Most people get it some people don't

Please help us spread the message!

Let's keep our children safe

## PALAGISSAFEKIDS

### SAFETY IS NO ACCIDENT

**"A Little Effort Makes a Big Difference"**

PALAGIS
ICE CREAM SHACK

Be our guest,
come visit us at
company headquarters
and receive one small
ice cream cone
and two small
lemonades,
Free on us.
A $7.00
value.

55
Bacon St.,
Pawtucket,
RI

www.ingramcontent.com/pod-product-compliance
Lightning Source LLC
Chambersburg PA
CBHW071344090426
42738CB00012B/3010